G000022350

THE MEDICAL DEVICE EXCISE TAX

SELECTED ANALYSES

HEALTH CARE ISSUES, COSTS AND ACCESS

Additional books in this series can be found on Nova's website under the Series tab.

Additional e-books in this series can be found on Nova's website under the e-book tab.

HEALTH CARE ISSUES, COSTS AND ACCESS

THE MEDICAL DEVICE EXCISE TAX

SELECTED ANALYSES

NINA KIMBALL-VERONESI
EDITOR

New York

Copyright © 2014 by Nova Science Publishers, Inc.

All rights reserved. No part of this book may be reproduced, stored in a retrieval system or transmitted in any form or by any means: electronic, electrostatic, magnetic, tape, mechanical photocopying, recording or otherwise without the written permission of the Publisher.

For permission to use material from this book please contact us:
Telephone 631-231-7269; Fax 631-231-8175
Web Site: http://www.novapublishers.com

NOTICE TO THE READER

The Publisher has taken reasonable care in the preparation of this book, but makes no expressed or implied warranty of any kind and assumes no responsibility for any errors or omissions. No liability is assumed for incidental or consequential damages in connection with or arising out of information contained in this book. The Publisher shall not be liable for any special, consequential, or exemplary damages resulting, in whole or in part, from the readers' use of, or reliance upon, this material. Any parts of this book based on government reports are so indicated and copyright is claimed for those parts to the extent applicable to compilations of such works.

Independent verification should be sought for any data, advice or recommendations contained in this book. In addition, no responsibility is assumed by the publisher for any injury and/or damage to persons or property arising from any methods, products, instructions, ideas or otherwise contained in this publication.

This publication is designed to provide accurate and authoritative information with regard to the subject matter covered herein. It is sold with the clear understanding that the Publisher is not engaged in rendering legal or any other professional services. If legal or any other expert assistance is required, the services of a competent person should be sought. FROM A DECLARATION OF PARTICIPANTS JOINTLY ADOPTED BY A COMMITTEE OF THE AMERICAN BAR ASSOCIATION AND A COMMITTEE OF PUBLISHERS.

Additional color graphics may be available in the e-book version of this book.

Library of Congress Cataloging-in-Publication Data

ISBN: 978-1-63117-598-5

Published by Nova Science Publishers, Inc. † New York

CONTENTS

PREFACE

As part of recent health care reform efforts, Congress, in the Affordable Care Act, imposed a 2.3% excise tax on the sale of certain medical devices by device manufacturers, producers, or importers. This book reviews the issues surrounding the medical devices tax within the framework of basic principles surrounding the choice of commodities to tax under excise taxes. It also describes the tax and its legislative origins. After that, the book analyzes the arguments for retaining and repealing the tax; provides a brief overview of the recently enacted Treasury regulations; analyzes the legal implications of the regulations; and answers frequently asked questions about the medical device tax.

Chapter 1 - The 2.3% medical device tax imposed by the Affordable Care Act (ACA; P.L. 111-148) in 2010 was one of a number of additional revenue-raising provisions to finance health reform. This tax, which took effect in January 2013, is projected to collect approximately $38 billion of excise tax revenues over the next 10 years, resulting in $29 billion of net revenues, after accounting for offsets from other taxes.

Some have called for a repeal of the medical device tax since enactment in 2010. Repeal of the tax has become such a high priority for some Members of Congress that it was one of the provisions discussed in the October 2013 negotiations over ending the federal government shutdown and increases in the federal debt ceiling. Repeal, delay, or reform of the tax could be included in future negotiations over the federal budget, debt ceiling, or tax reform.

The major justification offered for the medical device tax is its revenue, which helps offset the cost of the ACA. Although the tax is relatively small, no revenue replacement has been proposed and it may be difficult to find. There is also a concern among some that eliminating the medical device tax would lead to proposals to eliminate similar fees and taxes on other industries, the sum of which, including the device tax, totals $165 billion over 10 years. The tax was justified partly because the medical device industry was among the commercial interests that stood to benefit from unanticipated profits as more individuals enroll in health care insurance, post-ACA.

Viewed from the perspective of traditional economic and tax theory, however, the tax is challenging to justify. In general, tax policy is more efficient when differential excise taxes are not imposed. It is generally more efficient to raise revenue from a broad tax base. Therefore excise taxes are usually based on specific objectives such as discouraging undesirable activities (e.g., tobacco taxes) or funding closely related government spending (e.g., gasoline taxes to finance highway construction). These justifications do not apply, other than weakly, to the medical device case. The tax also imposes administrative and compliance costs that may be disproportionate to revenue.

Opponents of the tax claim that the medical device tax could have significant, negative consequences for the U.S. medical device industry and on jobs. The estimates in this report suggest fairly minor effects, with output and employment in the industry falling by no more than two-tenths of 1%. This limited effect is due to the small tax rate, the exemption of approximately half of output, and the relatively insensitive demand for health services.

The analysis suggests that most of the tax will fall on consumer prices, and not on profits of medical device companies. The effect on the price of health care, however, will most likely be negligible because of the small size of the tax and small share of health care spending attributable to medical devices.

Chapter 2 - On December 7, 2012, the Department of the Treasury and the Internal Revenue Service issued final regulations explaining the scope of the medical device excise tax created by the Health Care and Education Reconciliation Act of 2010 (HCERA), which modified the Patient Protection and Affordable Care Act of 2010. The new regulations were issued less than a month before the 2.3% excise tax took effect on January 1, 2013. This report provides a brief overview of the recently enacted Treasury regulations, analyzes the legal implications of the regulations, and answers frequently asked questions about the medical device tax.

The Treasury regulations on the medical device excise tax explain both who is subject to the excise tax and the scope of the statutory exemptions provided for the tax. Specifically, the regulations incorporate by reference the general definitions for a "manufacturer, producer, or importer" outlined in the Internal Revenue Code, meaning that the excise tax will be directly paid by manufacturers, as opposed to consumers or others that use a given medical device.

Furthermore, the regulations attempt to clarify the limits to the medical device excise tax. Beyond the statutory exemptions created for eyeglasses, contact lenses, and hearing aids, the law created a "retail exemption" to the excise tax, excluding from the tax medical devices that are "generally purchased by the general public at retail for individual use." The Treasury regulations attempt to simultaneously provide certainty to potential taxpayers as to which devices are subject to the retail exemption, while allowing the government the flexibility to properly apply the retail exemption to the variety of devices that could be exposed to the excise tax. The regulations provide a flexible two-prong test to determine whether a device should fall within the retail exemption, applying the exemption when the device is (1) regularly available for purchase by non-professional consumers and (2) not primarily intended for use by medical professionals. The regulations provide several factors to consider when applying the two-prong test. To provide some certainty to the scope of the retail exemption, the regulations also included several "safe harbor" provisions, explicitly acknowledging that certain devices, such as "over-the-counter" devices, fall within the retail exemption.

The new Treasury regulations on the medical device excise tax, while providing some certainty with respect to what devices will be exempt from the tax, generally favor a more flexible approach to defining the scope of the central exemption to the tax. As a consequence, uncertainty remains as to which medical devices will be subject to the tax. Indeed, Treasury, in releasing the medical device excise tax regulations, notes that further clarification on various issues implicated by the tax is still needed. As such, the regulations constitute only the first step in defining the limits of the medical device excise tax.

Chapter 3 - Report of the Internal Revenue Service on Medical Device Excise Tax: Frequently Asked Questions.

Chapter 4 - There are four common types of excise taxes: (1) sumptuary (or "sin") taxes, (2) regulatory or environmental taxes, (3) benefit-based taxes (or user charges), and (4) luxury taxes. Sumptuary taxes were traditionally imposed for moral reasons, but are currently rationalized, in part, to discourage a specific activity that is thought to have negative spillover effects (or "externalities") on society. Regulatory or environmental taxes are imposed to offset external costs associated with regulating public safety or to discourage consumption of a specific commodity that is thought to have negative externalities on society. Benefit-based taxes (which include user charges) are imposed to charge users of a particular public good for financing and maintenance of that public good. Lastly, luxury taxes are primarily imposed as one way to raise revenue, particularly from higher-income households.

This report provides an introduction and general analysis of excise taxes. First, a brief history of U.S. excise tax policy is provided. Second, the various forms of excise taxes and their respective administrative advantages and disadvantages are described. Third, the effect of federal excise taxes on federal, state, and local tax revenue is discussed. Fourth, the economic effects of various types of excise taxes are analyzed. The effects on consumer behavior and equity among taxpayers could be important issues for assessment of current excise tax policy or for the design of new excise taxes.

Excise taxes have generally played a diminishing role in financing the federal government since the middle of the 20th century for multiple reasons. First, Congress has taken legislative action to eliminate many categories of excise taxes. Second, most excise tax rates set in statute have declined in value over time due to inflation and inaction by Congress to change tax rates set in statute.

Excise taxes tend to be regressive, in that lower-income households generally pay a larger share of their income in excise taxes than higher-income households. Because excise taxes generally increase the price of the taxed commodity, they also tend to lower consumer demand.

Excise taxes play a much smaller role in financing the federal government than they did in the past. In 1960, federal excise tax collections were $355.49 billion (in 2012 constant dollars, after accounting for inflation). In FY2012, federal excise tax collections were $56.17 billion (roughly one-sixth of their 1960 value in 2012 constant dollars). Federal excise taxes comprised 7.0% of all federal revenue in 1973, whereas they comprised 3.2% in 2012.

Congress may be interested in revisiting the revenue and economic effects of excise taxes because these taxes could play a growing role in financing public goods. Some long-standing excise tax proposals to correct alleged social costs have resurfaced from time to time in policy discussions. Some of these proposals could be targeted towards specific products or activities (e.g., a "sugar-sweetened beverages" tax), while others could affect a broad range of economic activity and raise a significant amount of revenue (e.g., a carbon tax). On the other hand, there is also interest in reducing current excise tax rates as a means to encourage short-term growth in particular industries.

In: The Medical Device Excise Tax
Editor: Nina Kimball-Veronesi

ISBN: 978-1-63117-598-5
© 2014 Nova Science Publishers, Inc.

Chapter 1

THE MEDICAL DEVICE EXCISE TAX: ECONOMIC ANALYSIS[*]

Jane G. Gravelle and Sean Lowry

SUMMARY

The 2.3% medical device tax imposed by the Affordable Care Act (ACA; P.L. 111-148) in 2010 was one of a number of additional revenue-raising provisions to finance health reform. This tax, which took effect in January 2013, is projected to collect approximately $38 billion of excise tax revenues over the next 10 years, resulting in $29 billion of net revenues, after accounting for offsets from other taxes.

Some have called for a repeal of the medical device tax since enactment in 2010. Repeal of the tax has become such a high priority for some Members of Congress that it was one of the provisions discussed in the October 2013 negotiations over ending the federal government shutdown and increases in the federal debt ceiling. Repeal, delay, or reform of the tax could be included in future negotiations over the federal budget, debt ceiling, or tax reform.

The major justification offered for the medical device tax is its revenue, which helps offset the cost of the ACA. Although the tax is relatively small, no revenue replacement has been proposed and it may be difficult to find. There is also a concern among some that eliminating the medical device tax would lead to proposals to eliminate similar fees and

---

[*] This is an edited, reformatted and augmented version of Congressional Research Service Publication, No. R43342, dated December 23, 2013.

taxes on other industries, the sum of which, including the device tax, totals $165 billion over 10 years. The tax was justified partly because the medical device industry was among the commercial interests that stood to benefit from unanticipated profits as more individuals enroll in health care insurance, post-ACA.

Viewed from the perspective of traditional economic and tax theory, however, the tax is challenging to justify. In general, tax policy is more efficient when differential excise taxes are not imposed. It is generally more efficient to raise revenue from a broad tax base. Therefore excise taxes are usually based on specific objectives such as discouraging undesirable activities (e.g., tobacco taxes) or funding closely related government spending (e.g., gasoline taxes to finance highway construction). These justifications do not apply, other than weakly, to the medical device case. The tax also imposes administrative and compliance costs that may be disproportionate to revenue.

Opponents of the tax claim that the medical device tax could have significant, negative consequences for the U.S. medical device industry and on jobs. The estimates in this report suggest fairly minor effects, with output and employment in the industry falling by no more than two-tenths of 1%. This limited effect is due to the small tax rate, the exemption of approximately half of output, and the relatively insensitive demand for health services.

The analysis suggests that most of the tax will fall on consumer prices, and not on profits of medical device companies. The effect on the price of health care, however, will most likely be negligible because of the small size of the tax and small share of health care spending attributable to medical devices.

INTRODUCTION

The medical device tax was one of a number of additional revenues proposed to offset the cost of the Affordable Care Act (ACA; P.L. 111-148).[1] This excise tax is projected to collect $38 billion of excise tax revenue over the next 10 years. After offsets due to the deductibility of excise taxes from income and payroll taxes, the medical device tax is estimated to raise net revenues of $29 billion, according to official revenue estimates from the Joint Committee on Taxation (JCT).

While some wish to preserve this revenue source, others have proposed repealing the tax. The industry and some policy institutes have commissioned studies claiming that the excise tax will have significant negative consequences for jobs and innovation in the medical devices industry. Repeal of the tax has become a priority for some Members of Congress. The Senate also voted 79-20 to include repeal of the tax as an amendment to S.Con.Res. 8, the Senate Budget Resolution, on March 21, 2013.[2]

This report reviews the issues surrounding the medical devices tax within the framework of basic principles surrounding the choice of commodities to tax under excise taxes. The next section describes the tax and its legislative origins. After that, the report analyzes the arguments for retaining and repealing the tax.

A BRIEF OVERVIEW OF THE MEDICAL DEVICE TAX

Since January 1, 2013, manufacturers and importers of final medical devices for sale in the U.S. market have been subject to an excise tax equal to 2.3% of the manufacturer's price.[3] For the purposes of the tax, a "medical device" is defined by the Federal Food, Drug, and Cosmetic Act (21 U.S.C. §321(h)) and pertains to devices "intended for humans."[4]

Congress exempted eyeglasses, contact lenses, and hearing aids from the tax and any other medical device determined by the Secretary of the Treasury to be of the type which is "generally purchased by the general public at retail for individual use." The internal revenue code prohibits a tax from being imposed on the sale by a manufacturer of an article for export, or for resale by the purchaser to a second purchaser for export. Thus, medical devices manufactured in the United States and exported abroad are also exempted from tax.

The excise tax is deductible as an ordinary cost of business for firms subject to income tax.[5] If the tax falls on profits this effect reduces the tax, for profitable firms, to about 1.4%.[6] If the tax is passed forward, raising prices, the deduction would offset the firm's revenue gain from the price increase, leaving income tax revenues unchanged (absent effects on quantity) because the tax reduces the amount of income subject to federal income taxes.

Legislative Origins

The medical device tax was enacted by the Health Care and Education Reconciliation Act of 2010 (HCERA; P.L. 111-152), which modified the Patient Protection and Affordable Care Act of 2010 (ACA; P.L. 111-148). Like other revenue-raising measures enacted in ACA, the excise tax on

medical devices was meant to help offset the expenditures associated with
health care reform (e.g., subsidies for low-income households and small
businesses to purchase health care, and funding for programs to promote
efficiencies in the market for health care). Additionally, the medical device
industry was among one of the commercial interests (as well as health
insurance providers and pharmaceutical firms) that stood to benefit from
unanticipated profits as more people enrolled in health care, post-ACA.[7] These
industries are subject to fees.

This objective of the tax can be inferred from the original Senate proposal.
During the early stages of the health care reform debate in 2009, the House
and the Senate had different proposals to raise revenue from the medical
device industry. The Senate proposed an industry-wide fee based on a firm's
gross receipts, similar to the fees that were eventually imposed on drug
manufacturers and health insurance providers. In contrast, the House proposed
a flat excise tax across all medical device manufacturers; this framework
eventually was adopted during the reconciliation process for HCERA/ACA.
Even though the intent of the Senate bill might have been to impose the tax on
profits, a fixed dollar fee allocated by market share closely approaches an
excise tax.[8]

Revenue Effects

According to the Joint Committee on Taxation (JCT), the medical device
tax was estimated to raise $29 billion in revenue over the FY2013 to FY2022
budget window.[9] JCT estimates that the tax raised $1.7 billion in FY2013,
which would amount to approximately 1.4% of the sales of medical devices in
the United States.[10] This number is for a fiscal year, with the last quarter of
calendar year 2013 appearing in FY2014 receipts. The calendar year liability is
estimated at $2.4 billion.[11]

The excise tax collections are larger than JCT's net revenue estimates for
budgetary purposes.[12] Overall, excise taxes enter as a wedge between
aggregate output and income. Because these taxes reduce income, they also
reduce income and payroll taxes. JCT uses an offset to estimate net
collections, the offset being 24.3% for FY2013.[13] Consequently, the actual
revenue collected from the excise tax is estimated at $38 billion over 10 years
and $3.1 billion in 2013.[14] Based on these figures, CRS calculates that JCT's
revenue estimate projects a taxable base of $135 billion of manufacturers'
sales in 2013.[15]

ISSUES SURROUNDING THE MEDICAL DEVICE EXCISE TAX

In general, tax policy is considered more efficient when differential excise taxes are not imposed. It is generally more efficient to raise revenue from a broad tax base. Therefore excise taxes are usually justified on specific grounds.

Before discussing these justifications, it should be noted that the medical device tax tends to be a small share of the price of the taxed product, relative to other excise taxes. Most federal excise taxes are levied on a per unit basis, although a few are ad valorem (based on value, not quantity).[16] Fishing and hunting equipment is taxed at either 10% or 11% (except for tackle boxes taxed at 3%), transportation by air is taxed at 7.5% for persons and 6.5% for property. Large cigars are taxed at 52.75% (with a maximum of slightly over 40 cents). The unit taxes as an estimated share of value vary. Federal cigarette taxes are estimated to be around 16% of the retail price, but if measured on the same basis as the medical device and other taxes (before state and local taxes and on price net of the tax) the tax is more than 36%.[17] Although federal alcohol taxes vary considerably across brands, they are about 4% for wine and beer, and 8% for distilled spirits as a percent of retail price and would be higher on a comparable (net of tax and markups by distributors and retailers) basis.[18] A relatively small tax on medical devices means that economic effects are likely to be small, but also that administration costs relative to revenue are larger.

Arguments for Retaining the Tax

Revenue Needs
Taxes, among other justifications, are primarily for the purpose of raising revenues. One issue with respect to the medical device tax, and considerations of its repeal, is how the revenue loss might be offset, given current concerns about the deficit. The tax is relatively small, but, for political reasons, it may be difficult to find an alternative revenue source.

Perhaps more importantly, the medical device tax is one of a suite of taxes on particular industries adopted to finance the Affordable Care Act including fees on drug manufacturers and importers (estimated to raise $34.2 billion over 10 years), and fees on providers of health insurance (estimated to raise $101.7

billion over 10 years). These fees tend to have similar effects as excise taxes.[19] The "Cadillac" tax on insurers of high cost policies (estimated to raise $111.0 billion over 10 years) is also in the form of an excise tax.[20] The Cadillac tax becomes even more important in the future as it was delayed in taking effect. If there are justifications for eliminating the medical device tax, there may be arguments for eliminating these remaining taxes and fees. Those losses would present a more significant challenge in finding alternative revenue sources.

Taxing Industries that Benefit from Health Reform

A second argument offered for this tax (as well as the fees on other industries) is that the industry will benefit from the increased demand for their product due to the expansion of health insurance coverage in the health reform legislation. The tax might be seen as a way of reducing profits to the industry, as well as offsetting any negative effects of the tax on demand. The estimates of the economic effects of the tax, presented further in the report, suggest that the tax will probably not reduce profits, but will likely be passed on in price. It also suggests small effects on output and jobs, which probably would be more than offset by the expansion in demand.

Concerns About the Tax

Is the Tax Justified by General Rationales for Selective Excise Taxes?

Excise taxes have traditionally been collected for distributional effects, as benefit taxes (gasoline taxes which are used for highway construction and maintenance), and to discourage consumption (such as taxes on alcohol and tobacco).[21] Some of these arguments might be applied to justify the medical device excise tax. It is not the first tax to be imposed for purposes of reducing a one-time profit, as the windfall profits tax of the 1980s was in the form of an excise tax on oil.[22]

Some version of the benefit principle (that is, impose taxes on those who benefit from the spending financed by the taxes, as is the case with the gasoline tax) might apply as well. Almost all of the revenue sources in the Affordable Care Act were related to health. As a package, then, an argument may be made that taxes collected overall from consumers of health care might be appropriate to offset new as well as existing health insurance subsidies. Almost all individuals benefit from health care-related subsidies including existing benefits (from not taxing the value of employer provided insurance and Medicare, along with existing subsidies for Medicare and Medicaid) plus new benefits in the health law. The connection between the taxes and benefits, however, is very loose compared to the link between gasoline taxes and highway construction or taxes on firearms and ammunition and wildlife preservation. Some parts of the provision of health care services are not facing new taxes. It is difficult to explain the rationale for the tax based on the benefit principle.

Health care may be over consumed by individuals with health insurance who may face little or no cost of treatment, and often rely on doctors (who recognize there is little cost) to make these decisions. A tax might reduce this effect. The difficulty with this last argument is that the evidence suggests such taxes will be ineffective; they are not likely to alter the weak price signals that occur because consumers rely in part on decisions about their medical care and treatment made by physicians and other health professionals, and because that most of the cost is paid by insurance. This argument may be applied with the most justification to the "Cadillac" tax on excessive health insurance coverage.[23] There are also cases where more health care might be desirable, for example in lower income families where even a deductible or copayment might be unaffordable given competing demands on the budget. Thus the efficiency case for the tax appears weak and the tax may increase inefficiency.

In general, it appears that some justification for the medical device excise tax could be provided based on traditional economic principles, but the justifications, in most cases, are weak.

Administrative and Compliance Costs

One argument against the tax is that it imposes potentially significant administrative costs. While an extensive analysis of these costs is beyond the scope of this report, this section presents a brief overview.[24]

The medical device tax faces some of the same administrative costs as any other excise tax. Firms must: 1) determine whether they are liable for the tax; 2) determine that the product is the final manufactured good (i.e., no further manufacture will occur), and thus taxable; and 3) trace the supply chain and account for exempt purchasers.

In some ways, compliance with the medical device tax should be easier than compliance with other taxes. The only exempt purchasers involve exports (state and local governments and nonprofits are exempt purchasers of most other products subject to excise taxes).

Compliance may be more difficult than with other excise taxes in other ways. Because the tax is ad valorem (based on value) and some firms are vertically integrated (distribute as well as produce) or sell to related parties, those firms must construct a wholesale price, as that is the price on which the tax is levied. Most excise taxes are unit rather than ad valorem. In addition, although the medical devices tax falls on products already regulated and firms registered with the FDA (which can also share data with the IRS), there are exempt products. Aside from specific exempt products, a complication of the medical device tax is the retail exemption, which is open-ended and arguably unclear. This lack of clarity introduces a different type of complication compared to most other products subject to excise taxes.[25] On occasion, because of the heterogeneous nature of the goods, the final point of manufacture may not be clear (for example, in the assembly of kits, which is addressed in the regulations).

Very little has been written about the cost of excise tax compliance and administration. There is general agreement that taxing manufacturers rather than retailers or households is less costly and limits abuse.[26] One 1989 study in the United Kingdom found very small compliance and administrative costs, of about one-half of 1% of revenues.[27] This relationship would depend on the concentration of the industry (large firms can spread the administrative costs over more products) and the size of the effective tax rate. As discussed earlier, the tax rate for medical devices as a percent of manufacturer's sales is low, and the lower the tax rate, the lower the revenues relative to the value of industry output. Therefore, administrative costs may be higher as a percent of the tax for that reason.

Harmful Economic Effects on the Industry

One argument against the tax is the potentially harmful effects on the medical device industry, including a loss of jobs, a reduction in research and development, and harmful effects on smaller businesses. Some studies have estimated large negative effects from the tax (these are discussed in the **Appendix**). The remainder of this report estimates the likely effects of the tax on prices and output in the medical device industry. This analysis uses estimates of supply and demand response, along with the size of the tax rate itself and the exempt share to project effects on prices and quantity.

This analysis begins with an overview of the medical device industry. That analysis indicates that the industry faces different types of competition depending on product, and that about half of output is exempt from the tax (20% because of exemptions in the domestic market and 38% because exports are exempt).[28]

The next section of the report presents an analysis of the expected economic effects of the medical device excise tax. The analysis suggests the following:

- The tax is likely to be passed forward in prices, falling on consumers, not profits.
- The drop in U.S. output and jobs for medical device producers due to the tax is relatively small, probably no more than 0.2%. These small effects occur in part because the tax is small, in part because demand is estimated to be relatively insensitive to price, and in part because approximately half of production is exempt from the tax.
- With relatively small effects on the U.S. medical device industry, it is unlikely that there will be significant consequences for innovation and for small and midsized firms.
- To the extent that the tax does fall on profits, economic theory indicates that there would be no effect on output or jobs. Stockholders, however, would lose money, but that loss would be reduced because of device exemptions and income tax offsets. The tax on U.S. producers would be $1.2 billion in 2013 if the entire tax fell on profits.[29] The tax as a percentage of industry revenues would be 0.9%.[30]

Some of the technical detail of the analysis is in the **Appendix** which also contains a section assessing the estimates in other studies of economic impact that tend to project larger effects on jobs and output than the analysis in this report.

THE MEDICAL DEVICE INDUSTRY

The medical device industry produces a wide range of products. Some products have long been in existence and some are relatively new and are technologically advanced. Although there are a number of firms, output is concentrated in larger firms. Most large firms, both in the United States and abroad, operate on a global basis, and there are significant U.S. exports and imports. As a result, a significant fraction of the tax is projected to be paid on imports from foreign manufacturers (although some of those imports could be from foreign operations of U.S. firms, and some domestic production could be by subsidiaries of foreign firms).

Types of Products

The industry produces a broad range of conventional instruments and supplies such as syringes, needles, catheters, intravenous (IV) pumps, and surgical dressings. It also produces many advanced devices. An S&P Capital IQ ("S&P") survey identifies some specific areas where technologically advanced products have appeared.[31]

- In-vitro diagnostics accounts for about 14% of the global medical devices market and involves systems to test blood, urine, tissue and other bodily fluids. Most of the market is relatively developed although there are new advances in cardiac, HIV, molecular, and companion diagnostics (protein or genetic tests).
- Orthopedics accounts for about 13% of the global medical devices market, where joint replacements (mainly hip and knee) and spinal products are the main products sold.
- Cardiology accounts for about 12% of the global medical devices market, and includes rhythm management devices (such as pacemakers), implantable defibrillators (and similar items), ventricular assist devices, advanced stents, and heart valves.
- Diagnostic imaging accounts for about 8% of the global medical devices market, and includes X-ray equipment, ultrasound computed tomography (CT), positron emission tomography (PET), single photon emission computed tomography (SPECT), magnetic resonance imaging (MRI), nuclear medicine, mammography, and fluoroscopy.

Market Structure

The market for conventional products (such as catheters and needles), according to S&P, is characterized by close competition, with limited profit margins. Many large firms produce conventional items in addition to more sophisticated devices. Products with more advanced technology may face less competition and provide larger profits. While production tends to be by large firms, there are niches for smaller and mid-sized firms.

The top five global firms account for 28% of global medical device sales.[32] They include, in order, Johnson and Johnson, GE Healthcare, Siemens, Medtronic, and Philips Healthcare. Siemens is a German company and Philips Healthcare is a Dutch firm. The next five firms accounted for 13% of global sales: Abbott Labs, Covidien, Boston Scientific, Becton Dickinson, and Stryker. Covidien is an Irish firm (but was originally a spin-off from Tyco, a U.S. firm). The next five firms account for 7% of global sales: St. Jude, Baxter, Zimmer, Smith and Nephew, and Biomet. Smith and Nephew is a British firm.

Table 1 shows the distribution of U.S. firms whose principal activity is manufacturing medical supplies and equipment, based on analysis of corporate tax data collected by the Internal Revenue Service (IRS).[33] As seen in **Table 1**, while most firms are relatively small, most output is concentrated in the highest asset classes. The top 1% of firms (by asset size) accounted for approximately 80% of receipts in the industry in 2010.

Table 1. Distribution of Firms and Receipts for Manufacturers of Medical Supplies and Equipment from Tax Returns, 2010

Assets ($millions)	Share of Firms	Cumulative Share of Firms	Share of Receipts	Cumulative Share of Receipts
$0	18.4%	18.4%	1.4%	1.4%
$<0.5	59.0%	77.4%	1.2%	2.6%
$0.5-$1	4.8%	83.1%	0.4%	3.0%
$1-$5	10.4%	93.6%	3.6%	6.6%
$5-$10	1.7%	95.0%	0.8%	7.4%
$10-$25	2.0%	97.0%	2.1%	9.5%
$25-$50	0.9%	97.8%	2.3%	11.8%
$50-$100	0.7%	98.6%	2.8%	14.6%
$100-$250	0.5%	99.0%	3.7%	18.3%
$250-$500	0.3%	99.4%	4.2%	22.5%
$500-$2,500	0.4%	99.8%	21.6%	44.1%
$>2,500	0.2%	100.0%	55.9%	100.0%
Total	100.0%	100.0%	100.0%	100.0%

Source: CRS analysis of data from Internal Revenue Service, Corporate Sourcebook, 2010, Chapter 2, at http://www.irs.gov/uac/SOI-Tax-Stats-Corporation-Tax-Statistics.

Notes: Data from the firm size category of $0.5 to $1 million should be considered with caution according to the table because of small sample problems. There were 17 firms in the highest assets category, 41 in the next highest category, and over 9,000 firms in total.

Table 2 provides 2011 Census data on U.S. medical device production, exports, and imports, which can be used to derive domestic consumption.[34] As shown in Table 2, 38.5% of medical devices produced in the United States were exported abroad, and approximately 37.0% of U.S. consumption of medical devices was composed of foreign imports in 2011. In other words, it could be expected that 37% of excise revenues will be paid on products imported from foreign firms.[35] Note, however, that some imports could come from foreign operations of U.S. firms, and some U.S. production could be from operations of foreign firms in the United States.

Table 2. U.S. Production, Exports, Imports, and Domestic Consumption, 2011

Industry	U.S. Production	Exports	Imports	Net U.S. Consumption	Share of Tax Paid on Foreign Production	Share of Production Exported
		($ billions)				
In-Vitro Diagnostics	$11.5	NA	NA	NA	NA	NA
Electro-Medical, Electrotherapeutic Apparatus	$23.9	$10.3	$8.6	$22.2	38.7%	43.1%
Irradiation Apparatus	$5.7	$4.2	$3.8	$5.3	71.7%	73.7%
Surgical and Medical Instruments	$36.0	$15.0	$10.6	$31.6	33.5%	41.7%
Surgical Appliances and Supplies	$34.7	$9.5	$11.4	$36.9	31.0%	27.3%
Dental Equipment and Supplies	$4.6	$1.4	$1.6	$4.8	33.3%	30.4%
Ophthalmic Goods	$5.3	$2.0	$3.8	$7.1	53.5%	37.8%
Total	$121.7	$46.8	$43.9	$118.8	37.0%	38.5%

Source: CRS analysis of data from U.S. Census Bureau, International Trade Statistics and 2011 Annual Survey of Manufactures.

Notes: Data are by establishment. No data were available for exports and imports in-vitro diagnostics; it was assigned the average export and import share in the totals. Pacemakers and diagnostic imaging devices are included in "electro-medical, electrotherapeutic apparatus" categories. Diagnostic imaging devices could also be included in the "irradiation apparatus" category, depending on the type of imaging device. The North American Industry Classification System (NAICs) categories included in the order of rows in the table are 325413, 334510, 334517, and 339112 through 339115. These categories are also included in *Effects of the Medical Device Excise Tax on the Federal Tax Liability of the Medical Device Industry*, Ernst and Young (Prepared on Behalf of the Advanced Medical Technology Association), November 2012, at http://advamed.org/res.download

/14. Exports would be somewhat smaller (33% rather than 38%) if data on exports from trade statistics from the U.S. Department of Commerce and the U.S. International Trade Commission (at http://dataweb.usitc.gov/) were used Exports and imports may also reflect markups from distributors in the supply chain.

Some production is also exempt due to the retail and specific exemptions (eyeglasses, contacts and hearing aids), as well as a mark-up for distribution. Assuming a domestic market of $169 billion in 2013, this suggests that JCT's revenue estimate assumes that approximately 20% of the value of medical devices sold in the U.S. market will be exempt from the excise tax.[36]

As noted earlier, based on the data in **Table 2** showing the export share (which is exempt) and the analysis indicating 20% of sales are exempt through the retail exemptions, approximately half of U.S. production is subject to the tax.

ECONOMIC EFFECTS

The price and quantity effects of an excise tax as well as how the burden of the tax is potentially divided between above normal profits and consumers is driven by supply and demand in the market and represented in the slopes of those demand and supply curves.[37] Economists normally speak of *elasticities*, or the percentage change in quantity divided by the percentage change in price, when deriving demand and supply curves. In other words, elasticities measure the responsiveness of producers and consumers to changes in price. Any study of the effects of the tax contains explicit or implicit assumptions about these curves.[38]

Figure 1 depicts the market supply and demand curves assumed in this report's analysis, based on theoretical and empirical evidence. (For simplicity of exposition, the demand curve is presented as a straight line.) When a curve is relatively flat (nearly horizontal) it has a very high elasticity. When a curve is relatively steep (nearly vertical) it has a very low elasticity. In **Figure 1**, the market begins at an equilibrium price (P*) and quantity (Q*). The supply curve is horizontal. Making the supply curve very elastic makes output effects in the economy larger because it leads to the full pass through of the price. However, the market is also characterized by a relatively inelastic demand which causes a small effect on output. The demand curve is almost vertical. (These supply and demand relationships are discussed in the **Appendix**). The relationship in **Figure 1** would occur after adjustment to the tax has taken place, and would represent the steady state.

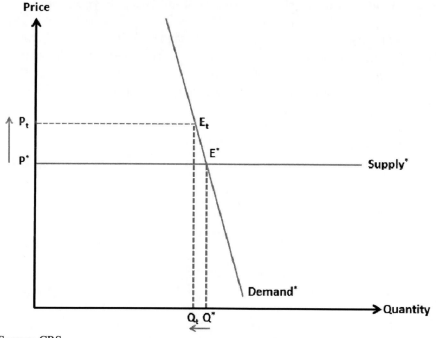

Source: CRS.
Notes: Q is quantity, P is price, and E is the equilibrium price and quantity point. Original values are marked with an asterisk. A t subscript indicates price and quantity after the tax.

Figure 1. Potential Effect of a Tax on the Medical Devices Market.

The following subsections discuss the evidence supporting a highly elastic supply curve and an inelastic demand curve.

Supply Responses to Price

The medical device market has not previously been subject to an excise tax, thus there are no previous studies that indicate how the firms in the industry react to a tax. Nevertheless, there is reason to believe that the supply curve for this industry is infinitely elastic or close to it in the long run, and therefore that the tax is passed forward into the price. There are several reasons to support this view.

First, as discussed earlier, much of the market, producing ordinary items such as needles and catheters, is described as competitive by the S&P analysis.[39] In the S&P report, which focuses on large publicly traded firms, there are 37 manufacturers of medical devices along with 11 additional firms that produce supplies, along with two other large firms that have a division producing these goods. IRS tax return data show over 9,000 firms producing medical supplies and equipment.[40] As shown in **Table 1**, even though production is concentrated at the top, there are still 17 firms in the top asset category and 41 in the second (see Note). In a competitive market, firms earn no profit above the normal return necessary to attract capital (if they did, other firms would enter to exploit it). Economic theory indicates that the market supply curve is perfectly elastic. Since these firms are price-takers, and are not influential enough to affect prices prevailing in the market, they will initially see their normal profits fall, and firms will begin to leave the industry. As quantity contracts, the price will rise (and rise relatively quickly if demand is relatively inelastic) restoring normal profits and stemming the exit of firms.

Second, to the extent that firms have market power, which may be the case for the production of more technologically advanced products, there is not a supply curve *per se* but an optimization of profits by firms that lead to some or all of the tax being passed on in price. As discussed in the **Appendix**, there are theoretical reasons that 100% of the tax could be passed on in price. The adjustment process could begin with raising prices or reducing quantity.

There is also a large body of empirical research on tobacco and, to a lesser extent on alcohol and fuel excise taxes that, while the findings are mixed, tends to indicate these taxes are passed forward in price and, in some cases, with more than 100% of the tax passed forward.[41] These taxes are per unit taxes, rather than ad valorem taxes (taxes as a percent of price), which could explain why more than 100% of the tax is passed forward (see the **Appendix**). Manufacture of cigarettes, in particular, is largely concentrated in a few firms.

There is one caveat to this standard analysis of supply. In the health market there are large purchasers such as hospitals, the federal government, and insurance companies that can exert market power. These buyers with market power could resist the pass through of price. However, even if these buyers have been successful in limiting the profits of medical device manufacturers, it does not mean the tax would not be passed on. For example, suppose the market power of large buyers is so great that all higher than normal profits that might be earned by medical device manufacturers are eliminated. Then these medical device firms are in the same circumstance as firms in a competitive market and must pass forward the tax in higher prices (which is a cost, just as wages are a cost) to stay in business. Or if there is market power but still some profits above the normal profit, the effect would be a more elastic individual firm demand curve which, as shown in the **Appendix**, should not affect price pass through.

There are some anecdotal stories to suggest that the tax is being passed forward.[42] In addition, S&P reported on a survey of firms in January 2013 that indicated 42% of firms (presumably large firms that S&P covers) were planning to increase prices, and the remainder had some type of cost cutting procedures in place.[43] Both of these activities are consistent with passing the tax forward in price (where producers can move first on either price or quantity).

Demand Responses to Price

In general the effect on output depends on both supply and demand. If the tax is passed forward in price because the supply curve is perfectly elastic, the effect on output and jobs in the industry depends on the slope (or elasticity) of the demand curve. The smaller the elasticity, the smaller are the effects on output. There is reason to expect that the demand curve for medical devices is relatively inelastic.

Medical devices are generally not final consumer goods, but are rather inputs into delivering health care services to individuals. An individual typically does not purchase a new hip joint directly from the manufacturer; he or she purchases a hip replacement procedure, which involves the joint, the services of doctors in diagnosing and operating, anesthesia, perhaps physical therapy, and other medical devices used in doctors' offices and surgery (e.g., needles, scalpels, and sutures).

The demand for a good that is an input into the provision of the final consumer service depends, in part, on the degree to which that input can be substituted for other inputs. (The derivation of the input demand curve is shown in the **Appendix**.) It is necessary to estimate how the firm using the good as an input (e.g., the hospital or physician) will change its demand as price changes. If all of the components (physicians' services, medical devices, drugs, etc.) must be used in fixed proportions, then the price of any one of them simply raises the price of the final good (e.g., the hip replacement service) by the tax rate times the share of the price that reflects the cost of the input. Thus, if 10% of the cost of the hip replacement is the cost of the joint itself, a 2.3% tax on the joint would raise the overall price by 0.23%. If expressing this effect in a demand elasticity, the sensitivity of the final consumer to price would be multiplied by the share of the medical devices in total health costs to get the firm's demand. For example if the demand elasticity for health were -0.5 and the share of devices in total sales were 10%, then the demand elasticity would be -0.5 times 10%, or -0.05. Elasticities can become very small for small inputs.

If other inputs can be substituted for the medical device, then demand for devices will respond to prices through this effect as well and demand for the medical device will be more elastic. The term for measuring this substitution of inputs in response to price is a factor substitution elasticity (percentage change in ratio of inputs divided by the percentage change in the ratio of input prices). As shown in the **Appendix**, the elasticity of demand for an input is the factor substitution elasticity times the share of other inputs plus the consumer demand elasticity for the final consumer product times the share of the input.[44] That is, the overall input demand will be the sum of the final consumer demand elasticity weighted by the share of the input in cost and the factor substitution elasticity weighted by the share of all other inputs in cost.

Factor substitution in the aggregate economy (between capital and labor) has been studied extensively. Although economists often use an elasticity of one (in absolute value) in simulation studies of the aggregate economy, empirical evidence has pointed to a lower value. One review of empirical studies places that aggregate elasticity at -0.5. Thus even the aggregate factor substitution in the economy is probably inelastic. The elasticity would be expected to be smaller in magnitude at the individual firm or industry level.[45]

Demand is less elastic for products with fewer substitutes. Thus, it is likely that the substitution elasticity between medical devices and other inputs into health procedures is extremely small, perhaps approaching zero. For a hip replacement, a joint is necessary, so the only response might be to choose a different type of joint. All joints, however, will be subject to the tax so their relative prices would not change. In addition, for many procedures there is likely little ability to economize on medical devices (for example, sutures), and also little incentive, where economizing is possible, when costs are charged to insurance and are less likely to affect doctors, who largely make these decisions.[46]

The overall demand elasticity for medical devices, therefore, requires an estimate of the consumer demand elasticity, an estimate of the factor substitution elasticity, and the share of medical devices in overall health services. One review of numerous econometric studies found the price elasticity of demand for health services, in general, to be -0.2.[47] If the factor substitution elasticity for medical devices is zero, the demand elasticity for medical devices would be -0.008, based on estimates that medical devices account of 4% of health costs (0.04 times -0.2 is -0.008).[48] It is likely to be smaller as more individuals become covered through health insurance since individuals with health insurance do not face the full price. (Note, however, that the share would vary by procedure. A higher share of the cost of medical devices would likely occur for a hip replacement than for hospitalization for an infection.)

Potential Effects on Output, Jobs, and Innovation

This section of the report analyzes the economic effects of the medical device tax under three sets of assumptions that provide sensitivity to elasticity estimates. First, the analysis considers both no pass through and full pass through of the price, which are the measures that define the possible values of the supply curve elasticity (zero and infinity). If there is no pass through of the tax, there is no effect on consumers and no change in quantity. As noted above the evidence does not appear to support this case. If some of the tax is absorbed by the firm, the firm must have above normal profits, and these profits above the amount required to attract capital will fall.

In the case of full pass through, which appears more likely and where the demand response is relevant, two elasticity assumptions are considered. Both assume that final consumer demand is - 0.2. In one, inputs into health services are assumed to be in fixed proportions, the factor substitution elasticity is zero and the demand elasticity is very small, -0.008. In the second case, the factor substitution elasticity is set at the same level as the consumer demand elasticity for health services, -0.2, inelastic and below the economy-wide average, but above the fixed input assumption. This assumption produces a demand elasticity of -0.2 and the demand elasticity set at -0.2. When this last assumption is made, the share of the cost attributable to medical devices is not relevant since both elasticities are the same. The demand may be more elastic for these technologically advanced products which may be a larger part of cost in the lower elasticity case, but there is somewhat more of a possibility that all of the price will not be passed forward, which has overall offsetting effects.

The range of effects from these cases is shown in **Table 3**. With no pass through of the tax in price, there are no effects on output, employment or innovation, since the tax presumably falls on profits. (As noted above, this outcome does not appear realistic.) The effect on profit as a percentage of revenue is reduced because only half of devices are taxed and because of savings in income taxes due to deductions for excise taxes paid. With pass through and inputs fixed and an overall 0.008 demand elasticity the factor substitution elasticity set at zero, the percentage reduction in output for U.S. medical device firms is estimated at 1/100 of 1%.[49] With the factor substitution and overall demand elasticity set at -0.2, the effect is estimated at two-tenths of 1%.[50] The results in **Table 3** when the tax is passed on in profit indicate a range of effects on jobs of almost zero to about 1,200.

Table 3. Projected Effects of the Medical Device Tax on Profits, Output, and Jobs in the U.S. Medical Device Industry

Possible Scenario	Effects on Profits	Effects on Output	Effects on Jobs
Case 1: Medical Device Companies Bear the Entire Burden of the Taxa	Profits fall by 0.9% of revenues	No effect	No effect
Case 2: Consumers Bear Burden of the Tax, and are Less Responsive to Price Increasesb	No effect	Decline of 1/100 of 1%	Job loss of 47 workers (0.01% of industry jobs)
Case 3: Consumers Bear Burden of the Tax, and are More Responsive to Price Increasesc	No effect	Decline of 2/10 of 1%	Job loss of 1,200 (0.2% of industry jobs)

Source: CRS estimates.

a Case 1 assumes no price pass through to consumers due to the tax.

b Case 2 assumes full price pass though, factor substitution elasticity is set at zero, and product demand elasticity is set at -0.2.

c Case 3 assumes full price pass though, factor substitution elasticity is set at -0.2, and product demand elasticity is set at -0.2.

These elasticities would determine effects on jobs (since there are no changes in relative factor prices for the medical device industry). For the factor substitution elasticity of zero, the job loss is 47, 1/100 of a percent of industry jobs. The effects for the -0.2 elasticity are 1,200 jobs or two-tenths of 1%. These relatively modest effects occur partly because the tax is relatively small, partly because half of output is exempt, and partly because demand is inelastic.[51]

Additionally, some have claimed that the medical device tax will lead companies to offshore operations and reduce employment in the United States as a means to avoid the tax.[52] The tax should have no effect on production location decisions, since both domestically manufactured and imported medical devices are subject to the excise tax.

A number of concerns have been raised about the effects of the tax on research and innovation in the medical device industry. The relatively small effects on the industry suggest that innovation and research would be minimally affected.

Claims have also been made that the small firms in the medical device industry will be disproportionately affected by the excise tax. Particularly, critics of the tax argue that small firms will reduce innovation as cuts to thin profit margins will lead them to reduce investment in research. These critics often note the large share of firms that are small, arguing that smaller firms have greater expenditures on research. They also indicate that smaller firms' profit margins tend to be small.[53] The analysis in this report suggests the effects on small as well as large firms will likely be minimal because the tax is expected to be passed on in price and the decrease in demand would be negligible. As in the case of virtually all industries, the share of firms is concentrated in smaller firms but output and research are concentrated in large ones. As measured by research and experimentation (R&E) credits (reflected in the general business credit)[54] most of the research and development is performed by large firms. The 17 firms with assets of more than $2.5 billion reported in **Table 1** are responsible for 56% of the revenues as well as 56% of the general business credit. Combining these firms with the 41 firms in the next category, firms with over $500 million of assets account for 77% of output and 80% of the R&E credit. While it is true that smaller firms (in part because they are new) have smaller profit margins, in most asset categories, firms tend to have net profits (even for tax purposes) that are larger than net deficits.[55]

In discussing innovation in the medical device industry, it is important to note that innovation for innovation's sake does not always lead to the most efficient economic growth path in the health care industry. Some have argued that the rapid adoption for high-technology equipment and medical procedures has been a significant contributor to rising health care costs in the past.[56]

While these technologies could offer absolute gains, in terms of quality-of-life and life expectancy, it is likely that the marginal cost of these new technologies begins to grow at a faster rate than the marginal benefits— resulting in higher costs for smaller gains.

In summary, the analysis in this section suggests that the effects of the current tax on the medical device industry should be relatively small because of the inelastic demand, probably no more than 1,200 employees should lose their jobs in that industry, and industry output and employment should likely decline by no more than two-tenths of a percent. While such losses directly impact the employees and employers, they are negligible for the economy (about 1/1,000 of a percent of the total labor force).

At the same time, one of the popular arguments for retaining the tax (that it will fall on profits of manufacturers), while still possible, appears unlikely. The nature of the industry, profit optimization, and some empirical evidence together suggest that most of the tax will be passed on to consumers in price. Some of this tax will fall on the federal government, which provides financing for some medical care. Even though there may be an expansion in demand that produces additional profits, a tax may be only partly able to offset it.

APPENDIX. TECHNICAL EXPLANATIONS AND STUDY REVIEWS

This appendix provides a more technical discussion and a derivation of the relationships used to capture supply and demand in this report. It is intended for the reader who is knowledgeable about economics. Three topics are addressed. The first is an exposition of the supply and demand relationships and how they can be expressed as relationships between the tax, price and quantity. The second presents a discussion of profit maximization with monopoly power (assuming the firm is in an industry characterized by market power). The final section discusses the derivation of the demand function for an intermediate good.

In this appendix, the following notation is used: P (price), Q (quantity), Ed (absolute value of the demand elasticity), Es (supply elasticity) t (tax), c (marginal cost), and S (absolute value of the factor substitution elasticity). A percentage change in x is dx/x. A change in the tax is dt, equal to the tax rate.

Supply and Demand Relationships

Figure A-1 presents the basic supply and demand relationship, showing the shift in price (from P^* to P_t) with a unit tax of t, and the shift in quantity from Q^* to Q_t. The net producer price, after the tax is imposed, is indicated by P_t - t. To simplify, linear demand and supply curves are provided and a per unit rather than an ad valorem tax (imposed as a percentage of price) tax are presented, although in the derivations an ad valorem tax is assumed. For this purpose there is no difference between the two.

To determine the formulas for price and quantity: The demand relationship is:

$$dQ/Q = -Ed\ (dP/P) \qquad (1)$$

The supply relationship where tax is imposed on P, and the net price is $P(1-t)$:

$$dQ/Q = Es\ (dP/P- dt/(1-t)) \qquad (2)$$

To solve for dP/P, equate (1) and (2) (since the change in supply and demand must be equal) and assume the initial value of t is zero, to obtain:

$$dP/P = (Es/(Es+Ed))\ dt \qquad (3)$$

To derive the change in output, substitute (3) into (1) to obtain:

$$dQ/Q = -(EdEs/(Ed+Es))\ dt \qquad (4)$$

If Es is infinitely large the value Es/(Es+Ed) becomes one, the supply curve is horizontal, and the entire tax is passed on in price, as shown in **Figure A-2**, on the next page.

With an infinitely elastic supply curve, output change is determined by the slope of the demand curve.

Contrast the effect on quantity change in **Figure A-3**, which has a much more inelastic demand curve.

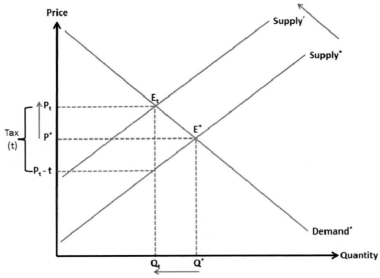

Source: CRS.

Figure A-1. Tax Adjustment in the Market.

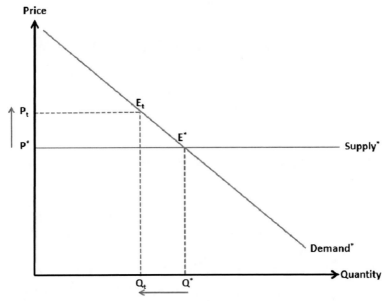

Source: CRS.

Figure A-2. Market Equilibrium with an Infinitely Elastic Supply Curve.

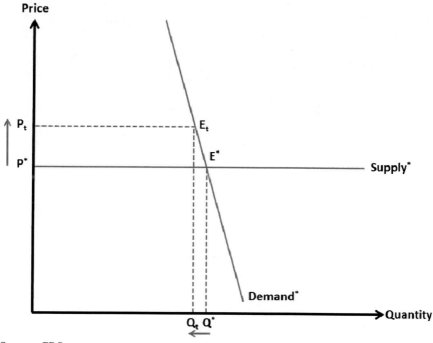

Source: CRS.

Figure A-3. Market Equilibrium with an Infinitely Elastic Supply Curve and a
Relatively Inelastic Demand Curve.

Figure A-3 is the basic type of relationship that analysis and empirical
evidence suggest may characterize the medical device market.

Price Pass Through for a Firm with Market Power and Above-Normal Profits

The two extremes of market structure are perfect competition and
monopoly. Most market structures lie somewhere in between. In perfect
competition, the supply curve is perfectly elastic as increases in output are
achieved by new firms entering the industry. Firms have no profits and are
price takers (i.e., cannot influence price) and ultimately must pass on any
excise tax in cost. Even market structures where there is imperfect competition
will still not have profits above the normal return as long as there is entry.

Monopolies rarely exist and they are typically regulated. However, firms
may have market power if there are barriers to entry. In this case, an individual

firm can be depicted as having a downward sloping demand curve as in the case of a monopolist selling a similar or a differentiated good. Each firm assumes its market conditions are not affected by others, although a contraction in output by one firm, with aggregate demand fixed in the overall market, will expand demand for other firms. This analysis examines the optimization process for an ad valorem tax in a firm facing a downward sloping demand curve. For a firm with market power, it is reasonable to assume a constant marginal cost (whereas a natural monopoly, such a cable company, tends to have a downward sloping marginal cost curve). A constant marginal cost assumes that firms have constant returns to scale and can produce additional amounts at the same cost. A rising marginal cost curve could also be considered, but it would not change the outcome for passing through the tax.

The firm's profits (H):

$$\Pi = P(Q)Q(1\text{-}t) - cQ \tag{5}$$

To totally differentiate this equation and obtain the maximum profit, given t:

$$(PdQ + QdP)(1\text{-}t) - cdQ = 0 \tag{6}$$

This analysis considers a constant elasticity of demand function:

$$Q = AP^{-Ed} \tag{7}$$

For this function,

$$dQ/Q = -Ed\ (dP/P), \tag{8}$$

or

$$dP = -(1/Ed)(P/Q)dQ \tag{9}$$

Substitute (9) into (6) and solve for P:

$$P = (Ed/(Ed\text{-}1))c/(1\text{-}t) \tag{10}$$

Compare (10) with and without the tax and the result is that P_t, the price after the tax is compared to the price without the tax, or:

$$P_t - P = tP/(1-t). \tag{11}$$

Because the tax is an ad valorem tax, the price rises by slightly more than P_t; for a 2.3% tax, it rises by 2.35%.[57]

Textbooks sometimes teach that a monopolist passes on half of the cost of an excise tax to the consumer and the same analysis would apply to a monopolistic competitor facing a downward sloping demand curve. This outcome, however, is an artifact of a linear demand curve which must intersect the x and y axis.

To solve for the effect with a linear demand curve, the demand function is:

$$P = a - bQ \tag{12}$$

This function can be solved by substituting (16) directly into the profit function:

$$\Pi = (a-bQ)*(Q(1-t)) - cQ \tag{13}$$

Differentiating (13), holding t constant, and finding the profit maximum,

$$(a-2bQ)(1-t) = c \tag{14}$$

Solving (14) for Q and substituting it into (12) leads to the price equation:

$$P = a/2 + c/(2(1-t)) \tag{15}$$

With an ad valorem tax the pass through is equal to $(1/2) (t(1-t))*c$ which passes through ½ of the portion of tax on c and thus less than half of the total tax appears in price.

Although the use of a linear demand function is commonly taught in discussing the pass through of taxes (perhaps because it requires simpler mathematics or can be expressed graphically), it is an unlikely demand function. It results in a quantity equal to zero at a finite price, and a quantity equal to a finite amount at a zero price. It is difficult to imagine any utility function that produces a linear demand function. A criticism of the use of this linear demand and its special attributes was made forty-five years ago by

Bishop (1968), and Mixon (1986) also criticized textbook writers for continuing to use the linear examples.[58]

There are also demand curves of the log-linear type, such as:

$$Q = Ae^{-bP} \tag{16}$$

which is a log-linear function (when expressed in logs it is $\ln(Q) = \ln(A) - bP$).

Without repeating the estimates, this function passes through the amount of the tax on c. Although this function is a curve, it still crosses the y axis. If the log linear relationship is reversed, all of the tax is passed forward but the quantity becomes zero at a finite price; it crosses the x axis.

Given the findings with respect to the more appropriate curved demand curve used earlier, it seems more likely that the tax is passed forward in full.

The individual firms' demand curves are more elastic than the aggregate market demand curve. As all firms begin to raise prices, their individual demand curves will shift out due to the actions of other firms, so they will not have to cut production as much and will reach the smaller quantity reductions consistent with a less elastic aggregate market demand. Alternatively, if they begin to adjust by reducing output, the actions of many other firms also reducing output will contribute to pushing up prices (shifting the demand curve out) leading to the appropriate market response.

Derived Demand Elasticities

When a product is an input into further production for a final consumer product, as in the case of medical devices, the demand elasticity in the market must account for that.

For a constant returns to scale, constant elasticity of substitution production function, the first order conditions for choice of a given input Qi, as it relates to its price Pi and the price and quantity for the final product, P and Q, is, denoting S as the absolute value of the factor substitution elasticity's and A as a constant:

$$Qi/Q = A \, (Pi/P)^{-S} \tag{17}$$

Taking logs and differentiating:

$$dQi/Qi - dQ/Q = -S(dPi/Pi - dP/P) \tag{18}$$

To substitute for dQ/Q, note that dQ/Q = -Ed dP/P

Note also that the percentage change in output price is a weighted value of the percentage change in input prices. Since other input prices are held constant, (dP/P = a dPi/Pi), where a is the share of revenue paid to the Qi input. Substituting those values into (21) results in:

dQi/Qi = -[S(1- a) + aEd].   (19)

Discussion of Other Studies of Economic Effects

Several studies have been used to support claims that the tax would reduce employment, reduce incentives for innovation in the U.S. industry, and reduce overall economic output. One study also claimed, in addition to direct effects on the U.S. market, the tax could encourage offshoring of production. As suggested by the analysis in this report, any negative effects on supply and demand are likely to be small. Additionally, assertions that the medical device tax will encourage offshoring of production appear to have no basis in economic theory. These individual studies are reviewed in this section.

Three empirical studies of job effects have been widely-cited by opponents of the medical device tax:

- Furchtgott-Roth and Furchtgott-Roth (hereafter "F-R") in 2011,[59]
- Battelle Technology Partnership Practice in 2012,[60] and
- Ramlet, Book, and Zhong in 2012.[61]

The F-R study projects job losses of around 43,000. They begin with estimates of job effects using supply and demand analysis. A range of elasticities were considered: 0.5, 1 and 5 for supply, and -0.5, -1, -3, and -5 for demand. The result is a range of job loss from 2,300 to 23,000. They choose an absolute value of 1 for each, which is the equivalent of passing half the tax on in price and reducing output by on half of the tax change (thus output falls by 50% of the tax or 1.15%). The projected job loss from this analysis is 4,700. Their estimate is based on a lower work force size than the estimate derived above, but because of the larger elasticity and not recognizing that half of output is exempt, is four times the highest job loss estimated in this report. Their job loss of 43,000 is much higher because of an assumption that 10% of the industry's production would move abroad which accounts for almost 90% of the job loss. There appears to be no reason, however, to expect the industry to relocate because of the tax. This tax, as is the case with other excise taxes, is imposed based on consumption in the United States. As long as production serves the U.S. market, firms will be liable for the tax regardless of location. Based on their calculations, only with respect to the output effect from the supply and demand analysis, the domestic market would contract by 1%.

Overall, this study has significant methodological drawbacks because its demand elasticity appears too high in absolute value (although its supply elasticity is too low) and because there is no adjustment for tax-exempt sales. However, the impact of unsupported elasticities is minor compared to the assumption that production will move abroad.

The Battelle study doesn't mention the tax, but rather estimates the effects of a $3 billion loss of revenue from a hypothetical event. It is interpreted, however, as a study of the effects of the tax. They estimate a job loss of 38,000. This number includes the job losses of suppliers of the industry through an input-output analysis, and general economic effects on the economy through spending. For the direct analysis of the industry, they project a loss of 12,947 jobs.

To translate the value of the tax to a change in quantity implies an implicit composite effect of supply and demand elasticity of at least one (in absolute value). This combined effect in implicit elasticities is larger than the -0.5 in the F-R study and five times the largest elasticity calculated above, -0.2). In addition to the large elasticities, this approach implicitly fails to reduce the tax by exports, which account for 38% of output. The extension of the job loss in the industry to jobs of suppliers and the economy in general is not considered an appropriate way to analyze a tax change that would be offset by an alternate revenue source, or to analyze longer run effects of a tax.

It is important to note that this study does not claim to estimate the effect of the tax. Using the study to show the effects of the tax overstates the effect because its implicit elasticities are too large in absolute value, its measurement of the effect does not account for exports, and it is not appropriate to include multiplier effects.

The Ramlet, Book, and Zhong study is very similar to the Battelle approach except that they explicitly attribute effects to the tax. They project 14,700 job losses for the medical device industry in 2022 (10,500 in 2014), and 47,100 for the economy based on estimates of suppliers. They use regression analysis to relate the change in output to the change in jobs. They have the large implicit elasticity of at least one. Their measurement of the tax using revenue projections understates the tax because it is not grossed up by income and payroll tax offset used to project the revenue loss. Their measurement overstates the tax because it does not exclude the effect of exports; these partially offsetting effects overstate the tax effect by 20%. The same criticisms of the Battelle study (if used as an indication of the effects of the tax) can be applied to the Ramlet, Book and Zhong study.

In the end, based on CRS analysis, the job loss related to the tax is far less than the range projected in these studies. It is more likely to be in the range of negligible, or zero, to a high of about 1,200.

End Notes

[1] The tax was imposed by the Health Care and Education Reconciliation Act of 2010 (HCERA; P.L. 111-152), which modified the ACA.

[2] Bills that have been introduced to repeal the tax include H.R. 532 (Paulsen) and S. 232 (Hatch). H.R. 1259 (Maffei) would eliminate the tax and enact alternative revenue sources. For a discussion of the political background and the lobbying effort by the industry see Michael Hiltzik, "More on the Medical Device Tax: The Lobbying Bonanza," *Los Angeles Times,* October 3, 2013, at http://www.latimes.com/business/hiltzik/la-fi-mh-bonanza20131003,0, 4617480.story#axzz2iewhpfCM; Sarah Kliff, "How Obamacare's Medical Device Tax Became a Top Repeal Target," September 28, *Washington Post's Wonkblog,* at http://www.washingtonpost.com/blogs/wonkblog/wp/   2013/09/28/how-obamacares-medical-device-tax-became-a-top-repeal-target/; and "One Industry's Hold on the Senate," Editorial, *New York Times,* April 1, 2013 at http://www.nytimes.com/2013/04/02/opinion/one-industrys-holdon-the-senate.html?hp&_r=1&.

[3] Excise taxes based on the price of a good are referred to as *ad valorem* tax rates, in contrast to a fixed, per-unit tax rate. For more background on excise taxes, see CRS Report R43189, *Federal Excise Taxes: An Introduction and General Analysis,* by Sean Lowry. The tax is levied on the sales price of the manufacturer, the wholesale price; when manufacturers are also distributors, a price must be constructed. Thus some revenues of medical device manufacturing firms would not be subject to the tax because they reflect the revenues the firms is making is its role as wholesaler.

[4] For more information on regulations relating to the medical devices excise tax, see CRS Report R42971, *The Medical Device Excise Tax: A Legal Overview,* by Andrew Nolan and Internal Revenue Service, "Medical Device Excise Tax: Frequently Asked Questions," at http://www.irs.gov/uac/Medical-Device-Excise-Tax:-Frequently-Asked-Questions.

[5] Firms report their excise tax payments by filing a Form 720 Quarterly Federal Excise Tax Return to the Internal Revenue Service (IRS).

[6] The top federal corporate tax rate of 35% would reduce the tax to 1.5% because federal income taxes would fall by 0.8% of revenues (0.35 times 2.3%) and a small additional reduction would result from the savings in state income taxes.

[7] Sen. Richard Durbin, Remarks on the Floor of the U.S. Senate, *Congressional Record,* vol. 155, part 188 (December 13, 2009), p. S13134; Rachel Bade and Kim Dixon, "Talking About the Medical Device Tax," *Politico,* October 15, 2013; and Paul N. Van de Water, *Excise Tax on Medical Devices Should Not Be Repealed,* Center on Budget and Policy Priorities, October 2, 2013, at http://www.cbpp.org/cms/?fa=view&id=3684.

[8] See CRS Report R40648, *Tax Options for Financing Health Care Reform*, by Jane G. Gravelle, which traces the revenue choices in the legislative history and discusses them.

[9] Joint Committee on Taxation, *Description of H.R. 436, The Protect Medical Innovation Act of 2011*, JCX-45-12, May 29, 2012, at https://www.jct.gov/publications.html?func=startdown &id=4431.

[10] This calculation is based on the market forecast of $127 billion in sales. Espicom Business Intelligence, *The Medical Device Market: USA*, September 30, 2013, at http://www.espicom.com/usa-medical-device-market.

[11] This number was calculated by taking one-third of the estimate of $1.742 billion for FY2013 and one-fourth of the estimate of $2.562 billion for FY2014, averaging them and adding the result back to the FY2013 total for a $2.352 billion.

[12] In estimating the effect of an excise tax, the JCT assumes the tax is passed on in price to the taxed sector. Because revenue estimating conventions keep output and prices constant, prices fall by the same amount (although typically as negligible as a percent) in other sectors.

[13] See U.S. Congress, Joint Committee on Taxation, *New Income and Payroll Tax Offsets to Changes in Excise Tax Revenues for 2013-2013*, committee print, 113th Cong., 1st sess., February 12, 2013, JCX-5-13 (Washington: GPO, 2013).

[14] These figures represent sales to hospitals, doctors, the federal government, etc., *not* individual consumers. If the markup to consumers is used for the basis for comparison, revenue estimates would compose a smaller share of the purchases of medical devices in the United States.

[15] To adjust from net to gross collections, divide by (1-0.243); thus $29 billion divided by 0.243 is $38 billion. The base of the tax for 2013 is determined by dividing $3.1 by 0.023.

[16] Most excise tax rates can be found on the Internal Revenue Service Form 720. Taxes on alcohol, tobacco and firearms are collected by the Alcohol and Tobacco Tax and Trade Bureau and rates can be found at http://www.ttb.gov/ tax_audit/atftaxes.shtml Many excise taxes are levied on a per unit basis, but some are ad valorem (a percentage of price).

[17] The federal tax is $1.01 per pack. According to the Campaign for Tobacco Free Kids the average price of a pack of cigarettes is $6.03, with $1.82 in state taxes, see http://www.tobaccofreekids.org/research/factsheets/pdf/0202.pdf. The tobacco settlement payment which is the same as a tax is about 43 cents per pack as reported in CRS Report RS22681, *The Cigarette Tax Increase to Finance SCHIP*, by Jane G. Gravelle. When all of these taxes are removed the net of tax price is $2.77, and even this price is too high since it includes wholesale and retail mark up. So the tax as a percent of manufacturers' price is higher.

[18] Sales data were from Standard and Poor's Industry Surveys: Alcoholic Beverages and Tobacco, May, 2013. Data on federal tax revenues were from Alcohol and Tobacco Tax and Trade Bureau, Cumulative Summary, Fourth Quarter FY2012.

[19] See CRS Report R40648, *Tax Options for Financing Health Care Reform*, by Jane G. Gravelle.

[20] See Letter from Thomas A. Barthold, Chief of Staff of the Joint Committee on Taxation, June 15, 2012, at http://waysandmeans.house.gov/uploadedfiles/jct_june_2012_partial_re-estimate_of_tax_provisions_in_aca.pdf; and Senate Finance Committee, "The Affordable Care Act: More than $800 Billion in Tax Cuts," press release, June 29, 2012, at http://www.finance.senate.gov/newsroom/chairman/download/?id=ac4aec3b-1110-4311-9db5-0f9539797a33.

[21] See J. Fred Giertz, Excise Taxes, *Encyclopedia of Taxation and Tax Policy*, Ed, Joseph J. Cordes, Robert E. Ebel, and Jane G, Gravelle, Washington, DC, 2005, pp. 125-127.

[22] See CRS Report RL34689, *Oil Industry Financial Performance and the Windfall Profits Tax*, by Robert Pirog and Molly F. Sherlock.

[23] See CRS Report R40548, *Legal Issues Relating to the Disposal of Dispensed Controlled Substances*, by Brian T. Yeh, for a discussion of the Cadillac tax.

[24] Some idea of the specific issues associated with the medical device tax can be found in the final regulations, at http://www.gpo.gov/fdsys/pkg/FR-2012-12-07/pdf/2012-29628.pdf. An extensive discussion of the tax and regulations including the retail exemption, see CRS Report R42971, *The Medical Device Excise Tax: A Legal Overview*, by Andrew Nolan. Some of this issues briefly reviewed here are based on Sean W. Rutter, Understanding the Medical Device Excise Tax (MDET), Slideshow, PriceWaterhouseCoopers. May 9, 2012, at http://medsupplychain.org/pdfs/ SeanRutter.pdf, and John Monahan and Gary Purpura, Medical Device Excise Tax: Minimization and Compliance, Slideshow, Tax OPs, May 11, 2012.

[25] This issue is discussed in detail in CRS Report R42971, *The Medical Device Excise Tax: A Legal Overview*, by Andrew Nolan.

[26] See Government of Canada, *Excise Act Review*, February 1997, at http://www.fin.gc.ca/earev /eareve.pdf.

[27] Cedric Sanford, Michael Godwin and Peter Hardwick; Administrative and Compliance Costs of Fiscal Publications, Bath,1989. Some discussion and evidence from that study are available on line in Jonathan Haughton Measuring the Compliance Costs of Excise Taxes, Discussion paper 14, African Economic Policy, Funded by the U United States Agency for International Development, 1998, at http://pdf.usaid.gov/pdf_docs/PNACF305.pdf.

[28] The exemptions in the domestic market include the specific exemptions for eyeglasses, contact lenses, and hearing aids along with other goods ordinarily sold to customers at retail. Some exemptions might reflect markups in distribution. The 50% calculation assumes that some portion of the exports would have been exempt anyway, so the share taxed is 50%, based on 0.8 times (1-.038).

[29] Calculated as $3.1 billion times (1-0.39) times (1-0.38). The first multiplier accounts for income taxes and the second accounts for exports. This calculation assumes: a) that these firms had taxable income and allowing for the income tax offset, and b) that 38% of U.S. production is exported abroad (thereby exempt from the tax).

[30] Calculated as 2.3% times (1-0.39) times (1-0.38) times (1-0.2). The last term accounts for tax-exempt products.

[31] Phillip Seligman, *Industry Surveys: Healthcare Products & Supplies*, S&P Capital IQ, August 2013.

[32] These data are taken from Phillip Seligman, *Industry Surveys: Healthcare Products & Supplies*, S&P Capital IQ, August 2013. In a different list, Baxter was in the top five, moving Philips to sixth place. See Medical Product Outsourcing, *The Top Thirty Global Medical Device Companies*, July 30, 2013, at http://www.mpo-mag.com/issues/ 2013-07/view_features/the-top-30-global-medical-device-companies-564773/.

[33] Table 1 does not include firms whose major activity is the manufacture of diagnostic imaging or in-vitro testing devices.

[34] Data in Table 2 are by establishment whereas data in Table 1 are by firm. A firm may have many establishments with different activities. For example major oil companies are classified in petroleum refining, but they also extract oil. Establishments are generally engaged in the activities described.

[35] This share assumes that the share of otherwise tax exempt income is similar between imports, exports, and domestic production for domestic consumption.

[36] The medical device industry is not precisely defined. The 20% exemption and the job effects calculated subsequently are based on a study by Battelle, Battelle Technology Partnership Practice, *The Economic Impact of the U.S. Advanced Medical Technology Industry*, Advanced Medical Technology Association (AdvaMed), March 2012, at http://www.chi.org/uploadedFiles/Industry_at_a_glance/BattelleFinalAdvaMedEconomicImpactReportMarch2012.pdf. That study measured the industry at $150 billion in 2009, and assuming a growth rate of 3% would be $169 billion in 2013. There are a number of other estimates of the domestic market size, some that appear smaller such as the $127 billion in Espicom Business Intelligence, *The Medical Device Market: USA*, September 30, 2013, at http://www.espicom.com/usa-medical-device-market.This number is consistent with data in Table 2 adjusted for two years of growth. Epsicom appears to estimate lower numbers, at least for the global market, than other sources. Their global estimate was about 85% of the estimate of Johnson and Johnson, reported in Phillip Seligman, *Industry Surveys: Healthcare Products & Supplies*, S&P Capital IQ, August 2013. Business receipts from the firms in Table 1were $155 billion in 2010, and did not include in vitro diagnostics of at least $10 billion, based on Table 2. These data suggest larger numbers.

[37] Economists define "normal profit" as the profit necessary to attract equity capital. A high rate of return (in the form of accounting profits) in the industry does not necessarily imply profits above normal returns because normal profit must compensate for risk.

[38] The change in price as a share of the change in tax is the elasticity of supply divided by the sum of the elasticity of supply and the absolute value of the elasticity of demand. (Demand elasticities are negative.) The change in quantity as a share of the tax is the change in price times the elasticity of demand. (All of these effects are percentages.)

[39] Phillip Seligman, *Industry Surveys: Healthcare Products & Supplies*, S&P Capital IQ, August 2013.

[40] Internal Revenue Service, Corporate Sourcebook, 2010, Chapter 2, at http://www.irs.gov/uac/SOI-Tax-StatsCorporation-Tax-Statistics.

[41] Some of these studies use differences in state taxes to estimate the pass through and generally, in the cases where they find the producer absorbing part of the tax, it is near the borders where customers from high tax states could purchase in neighboring lower tax states. While these state taxes are collected at retail, most retail businesses operate in a competitive environment which suggests that when part of the tax is not passed on, it is most likely ultimately absorbed by the manufacturer. For recent studies and literature reviews that indicate the tax is largely passed forward in price, see Matthew Harding, Ephraim Leibtag, and Michael F. Lovenheim, The Heterogeneous Geographic and Socioeconomic Incidence of Cigarette Taxes: Evidence from Nielsen Homescan Data, *American Economic Journal: Economic Policy* 2012, 4(4): 169–198, at http://www.stanford.edu/~mch/resources/Harding_CigaretteTaxes.pdf and *The Heterogeneous Geographic and Socioeconomic Incidence of Cigarette and Beer Taxes: Evidence from Nielsen Homescan Data*, March 2010, at http://www.cemmap.ac.uk /resources/scanner_data/sd10_harding.pdf; Douglas J. Young and Agnieszka Bieli´nska–Kwapisz, "The Incidence of Tobacco Taxation: Evidence from Geographic Micro-Level Data," *National Tax Journal*, vol. LV, no. 1, March 2002. Other empirical work finds the federal excise tax more likely to be passed on than state taxes, see P.G. Barnett, T.E. Keeler, and T. Hu, T., 1995, in "Oligopoly Structure and the Incidence of Cigarette Excise Taxes," *Journal of Public Economics,* vol. 57, 1995, 457-470. For gasoline taxes, the literature is more sparse, but one study finds half the federal tax and all of the state tax passed forward. Hayley Chouinard and Jeffrey M Perloff, "Incidence of Federal and State Gasoline Taxes." *Economics Letters*, Volume 83, Issue 1, April 2004,

Pages 55-60, at http://are.berkeley.edu/~jperloff/PDF/gastax.pdf. For studies that find that the gasoline excise tax passed forward, see James Alm, Edward Sennoga and Mark Skidmore, *Perfect Competition, Spatial Competition and Tax Incidence in the Retail Gasoline Market*, Fiscal Research Center Report No. 112, September 2005, at http://aysps.gsu.edu/sites/default /files/documents/frc/report112.pdf. Other studies generally find gasoline and diesel fuel taxes passed forward, but diesel fuel tax pass through is sensitive to supply conditions, see Justin Marion and Erich Muehlegger, *Fuel Tax Incidence and Supply Conditions*, National Bureau of Economic Research Working Paper No. 16863, March 2011, at http://www.nber.org/papers/w16863. A recent study suggests that diesel fuel taxes are largely passed forward, with greater passthrough the higher up the tax is in the supply chain. See Wojciech Kopczuk, Justin Marion, Erich Muehlegger, and Joel Slemrod, "Do the Laws of Tax Incidence Hold? Point of Collection and the Pass-through of State Diesel Taxes," National Bureau of Economic Research Working Paper 29410, September, 2013.

[42] Christopher Weaver, "Device Makers Add Fees to Cover Health Tax," *Wall Street Journal*, January 25, 2013, at http://online.wsj.com/news/articles/SB10001424127887323854904578264170779696696; Cathi Kulat, "Some Medical Device Manufacturers Not Paying Their Share of Health Reform," *The Hill*, October 19, 2012, at http://thehill.com/blogs/congress-blog/healthcare/301887-some-medical-device-manufacturers-not-paying-their-share-of-healthreform#ixzz2j9GfBNzI. Note that in the latter article that the author refers taxes on wheelchairs and canes as an example, but these items are *not* subject to tax under the retail exemption. Anecdotes also indicate that there is some resistance to passing the cost of the tax on to consumers. The "Medical Device Tax Watch" (http://www.devicetaxwatch.com/) is a website created by health care supply firms and other large purchasers of devices that publicly lists companies that are allegedly shifting the tax on to consumers. Note also that these instances are where firms have explicitly stated they are adding on the tax; firms may also simply raise prices without separately stating the tax. The Wall Street Journal article, cited above, suggests that the tax may be "baked in" to new contracts.

[43] Phillip Seligman, *Industry Surveys: Healthcare Products & Supplies*, S&P Capital IQ, August 2013.

[44] The absolute value of elasticity is $(1-\alpha)S +\alpha Ed$, where α is the share of the medical device in output, S is the absolute value of the factor substitution elasticity and Ed is the absolute value of the demand elasticity.

[45] Jennifer Gravelle, "Corporate Tax Incidence: Review of General Equilibrium Estimates and Analysis," *National Tax Journal*, Vol. 66, March 2013, pp. 185-214.A Congressional Budget Office working paper version can be found at http://cbo.gov/sites/default/files /cbofiles/ftpdocs/115xx/doc11519/05-2010-working_paper-corp_tax_incidence-review_of_gen_eq_estimates.pdf.

[46] Confidentiality clauses may also prevent physicians' knowledge of relative costs. Media reports indicate that some large purchasers are taking steps to help contain rising medical device costs. See Jaimy Lee, "Losing Preferential Treatment," Modern Healthcare, vol. 43, no.7, Feb 18, 2013, pp. 28-30. The more successful this change is, however, the less scope for responding to the tax by using a cheaper device.

[47] Su Liu and Deborah Chollet, *Price and Income Elasticity of the Demand for Health Insurance and Health Care Services: A Critical Review of the Literature*, Mathematica Policy Research, Inc., March 24, 2006, at http://www.mathematica-mpr.com/publications /pdfs/priceincome.pdf.

[48] Phillip Seligman, *Industry Surveys: Healthcare Products & Supplies*, S&P Capital IQ, August 2013.

[49] This is the elasticity of 0.008 times 0.80 (to reflect the share taxable) times 0.62 (to reflect the share exported) times 2.3%, the tax rate.

[50] This number repeats the previous calculation using the -0.2 factor substitution elasticity.

[51] It is also important to note, however, that these changes in jobs and output in the industry, even though they are small, do not reflect a reduction in output or jobs for the economy but rather a shift to some other sector. In the short run, economic analysis suggests that the economy would not likely be affected in the aggregate if the medical device tax were repealed and replaced by another source of revenue; rather, the location of employment would be affected. In the long run, economic theory suggests that there is no reason to view general job creation as an objective of government policies. Even if the workforce in the industry is reduced because of the tax, it is more likely that hiring slowed rather than firing took place. According to industry analysis conducted by S&P, demand for medical devices has been negatively affected due to slow economic growth and higher levels of unemployment in recent years. However, S&P forecasts that an aging population and higher health insurance enrollment (due to health care reform) will expand the industry's customer base in the United States.

[52] For example, see George Will, "Taxing Jobs Out of Existence," *Washington Post*, May 9, 2012, at http://articles.washingtonpost.com/2012-05-09/opinions/35454641_1_medical-devices-state-and-local-taxes-stryker; and Sen. Kelly Ayotte, Remarks on the Floor of the U.S. Senate, *Congressional Record*, vol. 159, part 42 (March 21, 2013), p. S2128, at http://www.gpo.gov/fdsys/pkg/CREC-2013-03-21/pdf/CREC-2013-03-21-pt1-PgS2053-7.pdf. However, media reports indicate that Covidien claimed that the decision was made on the basis of improving the efficiency of its operations rather than the medical device tax. See Zeba Siddiqui, "Covidien to shutter South Carolina plant, lay off 595," *Reuters*, September 13, 2012, at http://www.reuters.com/article/2012/09/13/covidien-plantclosure-idUSnWNAB119720120913; and Rick Foster, "Covidien denies layoffs report," *The Sun Chronicle*, May 11, 2012, at http://www.thesunchronicle.com/mansfield/covidien-denies-layoffs-report/article_a55f54db-b925-5b86-b246-136f2178e487.html.

[53] Katie Peralta "Small Device Companies May Bear Biggest Brunt of Controversial Tax," Wall Street Journal Market Watch Blog, October 10, 2013, at http://blogs.marketwatch.com/health-exchange/2013/10/10/small-medical-devicecompanies-may-bear-biggest-brunt-of-controversial-tax/; and Henry I. Miller, "ObamaCare's Medical Device Tax Will Cost Innovation and Jobs," Forbes, December 17, 2012, at http://www.forbes.com/sites/henrymiller/2012/12/17/ obamacares-medical-device-tax-will-cost-innovation-and-jobs/.

[54] Only the general business credit is reported in tax statistics for minor industries, but it is dominated by the R&E credit and R&E is the only credit likely to be claimed by medical device manufacturers.

[55] Calculated from data in Internal Revenue Service Statistics of Income, Corporate Sourcebook, Chapter 2, http://www.irs.gov/uac/SOI-Tax-Stats-Corporation-Source-Book:-U.S.-Total-and-Sectors-Listing. Taxable income tends to be smaller than financial profits before tax because of tax deductions, such as depreciation, that exceed economic depreciation.

[56] Although health care expenditures had been increasing at a rate greater than the growth of GDP for some years, recent data indicate that health care expenditures have been increasing at approximately the same rate as GDP growth in 2011. Explanations for decline in the growth of health care expenditures vary, and coverage of this issue can be found at Sarah Kliff, "Health care costs are growing really slowly. Americans haven't noticed.," *The*

Washington Post's Wonkblog, August 20, 2013, at http://www.washingtonpost.com/blogs
/wonkblog/wp/2013/08/20/health-costs-aregrowing-really-slowly-americans-havent-
noticed/; and "The Health Spending Decline," *The Wall Street Journal*, May 12, 2013, at
http://online.wsj.com/news/articles/SB1000142 4127887323744604578470752468155518.
For more general discussion on the role of technological innovation on health care costs,
and possible policy options, see the "Changing Incentives for Technological Innovation"
section in CRS Report RL33759, *Health Care and Markets*, by D. Andrew Austin.

[57] Note that had the tax been a unit tax, a fixed tax r, so that in equation (5) the tax would be
added to c rather than subtracted from revenues. In that case the price would go up more
than the tax: $P = (Ed/(Ed-1))*(c+r)$.

[58] Robert L. Bishop, "The Effects of Specific and Ad Valorem Taxes," *The Quarterly Journal of
Economics*, Vol. 82, No. 2 (May, 1968), pp. 198-218; and J. Wilson Mixon, Jr., "On the
Incidence of Excise Taxes on a Monopolist's Price: A Pedagogical Note," *The Journal of
Economic Education*, Vol. 17, No. 3 (Summer, 1986), pp. 201-203.

[59] Diana Furchtgott-Roth and Harold Furchtgott-Roth, Employment Effects of the New Excise
Tax on the Medical Device Industry, September 2011, at http://www.chi.org/uploadedFiles
/Industry_at_a_glance/
090711EmploymentEffectofTaxonMedicalDeviceIndustryFINAL.pdf.

[60] Battelle Technology Partnership Practice, *The Economic Impact of the U.S. Advanced Medical
Technology Industry*, Advanced Medical Technology Association (AdvaMed), March 2012,
at http://www.chi.org/uploadedFiles/Industry_at_a_glance/BattelleFinalAdvaMedEcono
micImpactReportMarch2012.pdf

[61] Michael Ramlet, Robert Book, and Han Zhong. The Economic Impact of the Medical Device
Excise Tax, American Action Forum, June 4, 2012 at http://americanactionforum.org
/sites/default/files/ The_Economic_Impact_of_the_Medical_Device_Excise_Tax.pdf.

In: The Medical Device Excise Tax   ISBN: 978-1-63117-598-5
Editor: Nina Kimball-Veronesi   © 2014 Nova Science Publishers, Inc.

Chapter 2

THE MEDICAL DEVICE EXCISE TAX: A LEGAL OVERVIEW*

Andrew Nolan

SUMMARY

On December 7, 2012, the Department of the Treasury and the Internal Revenue Service issued final regulations explaining the scope of the medical device excise tax created by the Health Care and Education Reconciliation Act of 2010 (HCERA), which modified the Patient Protection and Affordable Care Act of 2010. The new regulations were issued less than a month before the 2.3% excise tax took effect on January 1, 2013. This report provides a brief overview of the recently enacted Treasury regulations, analyzes the legal implications of the regulations, and answers frequently asked questions about the medical device tax.

The Treasury regulations on the medical device excise tax explain both who is subject to the excise tax and the scope of the statutory exemptions provided for the tax. Specifically, the regulations incorporate by reference the general definitions for a "manufacturer, producer, or importer" outlined in the Internal Revenue Code, meaning that the excise tax will be directly paid by manufacturers, as opposed to consumers or others that use a given medical device.

---

* This is an edited, reformatted and augmented version of a Congressional Research Service publication, CRS Report for Congress R42971, from www.crs.gov, prepared for Members and Committees of Congress, dated October 11, 2013.

Furthermore, the regulations attempt to clarify the limits to the medical device excise tax. Beyond the statutory exemptions created for eyeglasses, contact lenses, and hearing aids, the law created a "retail exemption" to the excise tax, excluding from the tax medical devices that are "generally purchased by the general public at retail for individual use." The Treasury regulations attempt to simultaneously provide certainty to potential taxpayers as to which devices are subject to the retail exemption, while allowing the government the flexibility to properly apply the retail exemption to the variety of devices that could be exposed to the excise tax. The regulations provide a flexible two-prong test to determine whether a device should fall within the retail exemption, applying the exemption when the device is (1) regularly available for purchase by non-professional consumers and (2) not primarily intended for use by medical professionals. The regulations provide several factors to consider when applying the two-prong test. To provide some certainty to the scope of the retail exemption, the regulations also included several "safe harbor" provisions, explicitly acknowledging that certain devices, such as "over-the-counter" devices, fall within the retail exemption.

The new Treasury regulations on the medical device excise tax, while providing some certainty with respect to what devices will be exempt from the tax, generally favor a more flexible approach to defining the scope of the central exemption to the tax. As a consequence, uncertainty remains as to which medical devices will be subject to the tax. Indeed, Treasury, in releasing the medical device excise tax regulations, notes that further clarification on various issues implicated by the tax is still needed. As such, the regulations constitute only the first step in defining the limits of the medical device excise tax.

INTRODUCTION

As part of recent health care reform efforts, Congress, in the Affordable Care Act,[1] imposed a 2.3% excise tax on the sale of certain medical devices by device manufacturers, producers, or importers.[2] The excise tax is effective on sales of devices made after December 31, 2012.[3] The implementation of the medical device tax has prompted some Members of Congress to seek a delay of the enforcement of the tax out of a concern that the "uncertainty and confusion" regarding compliance with the medical device excise tax will harm the medical technology industry.[4] Others in Congress have sought an outright repeal of the tax.[5] While December 31, 2012, passed without Congress changing or repealing the medical device excise tax, congressional interest remains.[6] On December 7, 2012, the Department of the Treasury (Treasury) issued its final regulations that provide guidance on both who must pay the excise tax and the scope of products encompassed by the excise tax.[7] This report provides a brief overview of the regulations, discusses the extent to which the rules have clarified the excise tax imposed on the sale of medical devices, and answers frequently asked questions about the medical device tax.[8]

ON WHOM IS THE MEDICAL DEVICE EXCISE TAX IMPOSED?

Pursuant to §4191(a) of the Internal Revenue Code (IRC), a "manufacturer, producer, or importer" making the sale of a taxable medical device is liable for a tax of 2.3% of the price[9] for which the device was sold.[10] Treasury, in the newly released regulations on the medical device excise tax, states that the "existing chapter 32 rules," including the definitions for "manufacturer," "producer," and "importer," apply with respect to the medical device excise tax.[11] In turn, the general chapter 32 rules define the term "manufacturer" as "any person who produces a taxable article ... by processing, manipulating, or changing the form of an article or by combining or assembling two or more articles."[12] Moreover, the general definition for a manufacturer necessarily includes the terms "producer" and "importer."[13] While courts have interpreted the term "manufacturer" within the general chapter 32 rules to encompass a range of activities where a person physically changes a taxable article, [14] the medical device excise tax, by definition, is not directly levied upon a consumer of a medical device.

WHAT IS A "TAXABLE MEDICAL DEVICE"?

The medical device excise tax created by the ACA is imposed on the sale of "taxable medical device[s]."[15] The statute defines that term by incorporating the definition of "medical device" from the Federal Food, Drug and Cosmetic Act (FFDCA), as that term pertains to a device "intended for humans."[16] Courts have recognized that Congress defined the term "medical device" in the FFDCA "very broadly,"[17] as the Food and Drug Administration (FDA) regulates a range of devices from tongue depressors[18] to artificial hearts.[19] As such, the Health Care and Education Reconciliation Act of 2010 (HCERA) casts a wide net with the term "taxable medical device."[20] In line with the broad scope of the term "taxable medical device," the December 7, 2012, Treasury Regulations explain that a "taxable medical device" is a device that has been registered with the Food and Drug Administration pursuant to Section 510(j) of the FFDCA[21] and 21 C.F.R. Part 807.[22] Importantly, Treasury resisted efforts by commenters to narrow the scope of the general term "taxable medical device," by limiting, for example, the term to devices that could exclusively be used by humans or could only be used for a medical purpose, preferring instead to maintain a broad reading of what devices are subject to the excise tax.[23] As a result, devices like infusion pumps, which can be used on both humans and animals, [24] and latex gloves,[25] which can be used for both medical and non-medical purposes, fall within the broad definition of a "taxable medical device."

MEDICAL DEVICES EXEMPTED FROM THE EXCISE TAX

In an effort to limit the ambit of the excise tax imposed on medical device manufacturers, Congress explicitly excluded three types of devices from the term "taxable medical device" in IRC §4191(a).[26] Specifically, Congress exempted eyeglasses, contact lenses, and hearing aids from the excise tax.[27] Moreover, the statute empowers the Secretary of the Treasury under the "retail exemption" to exempt "any other medical device" which is determined to be of a "type which is generally purchased by the general public at retail for individual use" from the 2.3% excise tax.[28]

The Retail Exemption

The regulations issued by Treasury on December 7, 2012, provide a broad framework as to which medical devices fall within the "retail exemption" to the excise tax under IRC §4191(b)(2)(d). Specifically, the new Treasury regulations provide a two-prong test to resolve whether a device should fall within the residual exception to the excise tax.[29] First, the device in question should be "regularly available for purchase and use by individual consumers who are not medical professionals." Second, the device's design should "demonstrate[] that it is not primarily intended for use" in a medical institution, office, or by a medical professional.[30] Neither prong is dispositive to the determination, as the regulations caution that an analysis of whether a device fits within the retail exemption is dependent on "all" "relevant facts and circumstances."[31]

To guide the analysis of whether a particular device meets the relevant requirements for the retail exemption, the new Treasury regulations provide a host of factors to examine.[32] Factors implicating the question of whether a device is regularly available for purchase by individual consumers include (1) the ability of end consumers to purchase the device in person through a drug store or other retailer that primarily sells a particular device; (2) the need of a consumer to seek help from a medical professional to use the device safely and effectively; and (3) whether the device has been classified by the Food and Drug Administration as a "physical medicine device" for human use.[33] To illustrate, with respect to adhesive bandages,[34] an application of the multi-factor test would conclude that the device is regularly available for purchase by individual consumers. Specifically, while adhesive bandages are not a "physical medicine device," the product can be readily purchased at various retail stores and can be properly used without formal training from a medical professional.[35]

Treasury also issued a list of factors to aid the determination of whether a device is designed primarily for use in a medical institution or office or by a medical professional.[36] Relevant factors include (1) whether the device must be implanted, inserted, operated, or administered by a medical professional; (2) the cost of obtaining and using the device; (3) how the device has been classified by the FDA;[37] and (4) whether the device is one for which payment is available "exclusively on a rental basis" and is an item requiring "frequent and substantial servicing" as those terms are defined under Medicare Part B payment rules.[38] Returning to the example of adhesive bandages, the multi-factor test counsels that the product is not primarily intended for use in a medical institution, office, or by a medical professional. Specifically, using adhesive bandages does not require the aid of a medical professional, and bandages are inexpensive to obtain and use.[39] Moreover, adhesive bandages are not classified as a complex medical device or a device needing frequent and substantial servicing.[40] Coupled with the earlier conclusion that adhesive bandages are regularly available for purchase by individual consumers, the totality of the circumstances indicates that "adhesive bandages are devices that are of a type that" should fall within the retail exemption to the medical device excise tax.[41]

Notably, Treasury explained in issuing the medical device excise tax regulations that two potential factors—the packaging or labeling of a medical device and the nature of documents submitted to the FDA in obtaining approval of a device—are irrelevant in assessing whether a device should fall within the retail exemption to the excise tax.[42] As a consequence, a medical device manufacturer cannot hope to escape the excise tax, for example, by labeling that its product is "intended for retail use only."

The Retail Exemption's Safe Harbor Provisions

In contrast to the malleable multi-factor test that outlines the limits to the retail exemption, the December 7, 2012, Treasury regulations also include a list of "safe harbor" devices that necessarily fall within the retail exemption.[43] The purpose of the safe harbor provisions is to "provide greater certainty" with respect to which devices are subject to the retail exemption.[44] The safe harbor includes medical devices, like pregnancy test kits, that are described as "over-the-counter" (OTC) devices in the FDA's online database for *in vitro* diagnostic tests, the FDA's classification regulations, or the FDA's device registration and listing database.[45] In addition, the safe harbor includes certain devices that qualify as "durable medical equipment, prosthetics, orthotics, and supplies" for which payment is available on a purchase basis under Medicare part B payment rules,[46] such as therapeutic shoes.[47]

Examples of How the Retail Exemption Is Applied

The Treasury regulations conclude by providing 15 different examples of how the retail exemption to the medical device excise tax would be applied in practice.[48] The examples range from the aforementioned "adhesive bandages"[49] to "blood glucose monitors"[50] to "magnetic resonance systems."[51] Examples of devices that Treasury concludes "based on the totality of the facts and circumstances" fall within the retail exemption include "absorbent tipped applicators,"[52] "adhesive bandages,"[53] "snake bite suction kits,"[54] "denture adhesives,"[55] "mechanical and powered wheelchairs,"[56] "portable oxygen concentrators,"[57] and "therapeutic AC powered adjustable home use beds."[58] Treasury also concludes that "pregnancy test kits,"[59] "blood glucose monitors, test strips, and lancets,"[60] "prosthetic legs and certain prosthetic leg components,"[61] and "urinary ileostomy bags"[62] fall within the regulations' safe harbor provisions. In contrast, Treasury, in its examples, finds that the following devices, based on the totality of the circumstances, are not exempt from the medical device excise tax: "mobile x-ray systems,"[63] "nonabsorbable silk sutures,"[64] "nuclear magnetic resonance imaging systems,"[65] and "powered floatation therapy beds."[66]

THE FUTURE OF THE MEDICAL DEVICE TAX

Whether the new Treasury regulations provide the needed clarity to alleviate the "uncertainty and confusion" that some Members of Congress have feared that the new tax would engender within the medical technology industry remains to be seen.[67] To be sure, the medical device tax regulations, with their safe harbor provisions, clarify that generally devices recognized as over-the-counter devices will not be the subject of the tax, providing an easy to understand exemption to manufacturers, importers, and producers of such products.[68] However, the safe harbor provisions are narrow, and the regulations open-ended two-part test defining the limits of the retail exemption, while providing flexibility as to the scope of the exemption, naturally creates ambiguity with respect to which products are exposed to the excise tax, save those specifically exempted under the regulations. Moreover, the limits of the retail exemption, which are based, in part, on regulations that were not crafted with the retail exemption in mind, could prove to be either over or under inclusive of Congress's original intent in enacting the medical device excise tax.[69] Treasury, in the release of the final regulations, identified several issues raised by the medical device tax regulations that warranted the agency issuing separate clarifying guidance, including the treatment, for purposes of the medical device excise tax, of licensing software [70] and "kits."[71] Given the wide variety of items that are categorized as medical devices,[72] some may see a need for further clarification with respect to other medical devices, including potentially expanding the safe harbor provisions. As a result, the December 7, 2012, regulations could be only the first step in clarifying the application of a tax that the Treasury Department acknowledges "may present certain implementation challenges."[73]

Moreover, looming over all the questions about the implementation and enforcement of the medical device tax is whether Congress will repeal the tax.[74] On March 21, 2013, the Senate voted 79-20 on an amendment to the Senate's 2014 budget to repeal the medical device excise tax.[75] Nonetheless, in 2012 the White House threatened to veto a repeal of the medical device tax,[76] and in the wake of recent debates over the federal budget, the majority leader of the Senate expressed doubts with respect to the likelihood of an outright repeal of the tax.[77] In short, the future of the medical device tax is at best uncertain.

FREQUENTLY ASKED QUESTIONS ABOUT THE MEDICAL DEVICE EXCISE TAX

What Is the Text of the Law That Imposes the Medical Device Tax?

The excise tax on medical devices has been codified in the United States Code in section 4191 of Internal Revenue Code. That section reads:

a) In general. There is hereby imposed on the sale of any taxable medical device by the manufacturer, producer, or importer a tax equal to 2.3 percent of the price for which so sold.
b) Taxable medical device. For purposes of this section—
    1) In general. The term "taxable medical device" means any device (as defined in section 201(h) of the Federal Food, Drug, and Cosmetic Act) intended for humans.
    2) Exemptions. Such term shall not include—
        A. eyeglasses,
        B. contact lenses,
        C. hearing aids, and
        D. any other medical device determined by the Secretary to be of a type which is generally purchased by the general public at retail for individual use.[78]

What Is the Taxable Amount?

The tax is 2.3 percent of the price for which a manufacturer, producer, or importer sold the taxable medical device.[79]

What Is the Effective Date for the Medical Device Tax?

The medical device tax applies to sales made after December 31, 2012.[80]

Can the Tax Be Imposed on a Contract to Purchase a Medical Device That Was Agreed to Prior to January 1, 2013?

The regulations provide some transition relief with respect to certain long-term contracts. Specifically, payments made on or after January 1, 2013 for contracts entered into before March 30, 2010 are not subject to the medical device excise tax unless the contract was materially modified on or after March 30, 2010.[81]

Where Do the Funds That Are Collected Go as a Result of the Medical Device Excise Tax?

The funds from the medical device tax go into the general treasury. The law that created the medical device excise tax, HCERA, did not contain any language regarding the disposition of the funds collected from the tax.[82] Without any specific overriding language governing with respect to the disposition of the funds, the Miscellaneous Receipts Statute would control.[83] That statute provides that generally "an official or agent of the Government receiving money for the Government from any source shall deposit the money in the Treasury as soon as practicable without deduction for any charge or claim."[84]

As such, without any other authorization, the Internal Revenue Service, upon collecting the medical device tax, must deposit all funds received in the general fund of the Treasury as a miscellaneous receipt.[85]

Is There a Complete List of Taxable Medical Devices?

The medical device tax is imposed on manufacturers, producers, or importers of a medical device that is intended for humans.[86] The Treasury's regulations interpret such medical devices as those that are listed with the FDA under section 510(j) of the FFDCA and 21 CFR part 807.[87] This list is quite broad and open-ended,[88] and, as such, the tax applies generally to all devices intended for humans subject to certain exemptions and exclusions, such as the retail exemption.

Is There a Complete List of Medical Devices That Are Not Subject to the Tax?

The statute imposing the medical device tax lists three specific devices that are not subject to the tax: eyeglasses, contact lenses, and hearing aids.[89] The statute also exempts "any other medical device determined by the Secretary to be of a type which is generally purchased by the general public at retail for individual use."[90]

Treasury regulations have provided examples of devices that would generally fall into the open-ended retail exemption.[91] Examples that Treasury has provided with respect to devices that are exempt from the tax are: absorbent tipped applicators, adhesive bandages, snake bite suction kits, denture adhesives, pregnancy test kits, blood glucose monitors, test strips, and lancets, prosthetic legs, endoskeletal shin systems, mechanical and powered wheelchairs, portable oxygen concentrators, urinary ileostomy bags, and powered adjustable home use beds.[92]

In addition, the FDA has provided a list of certain "safe harbor" items that fall within the retail exemption.[93] Nonetheless, because of the malleable nature of the retail exemption, there is no complete list of medical devices that are not subject to the excise tax.

Are There Reporting Requirements for Entities That Have to Pay the Tax?

Just as with other excise taxes, in order to report the tax liability to the government and pay the tax, those that are required to pay the medical device tax generally must file a quarterly return with the Internal Revenue Service using form 720.[94]

In addition, section 40.6302(c)-1(a) of the Excise Tax Procedural Regulations generally requires entities that are liable for excise taxes to make semimonthly deposits of tax during the period in which the tax liability is incurred.[95]

Generally under section 6656 of the Internal Revenue Code, failure to deposit the requisite tax subjects delinquent taxpayers to certain penalties.[96] However, the Internal Revenue Service has waived such penalties for the first three quarters of 2013.[97]

Will The Medical Device Tax Appear on a Line Item on a Consumer Receipt?

The medical device tax does not regulate what can or cannot appear on a consumer receipt for a medical device. Nonetheless, because of the retail exemption to the medical device tax, it would be unlikely for the medical device tax to be imposed on a good that is sold to the general public at retail.[98] In recent months, customers of the sporting goods chain Cabela's have circulated images of a receipt indicating that the company was imposing an additional charge on customer receipts for a "medical excise tax."[99] The charge imposed by Cabela's was reportedly the result of a software glitch and was not the product of any mandate imposed by HCERA's imposition of the medical device excise tax.[100]

Did HCERA, in Addition to Imposing a Medical Device Tax, Also Impose Excise Taxes on Other Items, Such as Sporting Equipment?

E-mails have been circulated suggesting that HCERA also imposed excise taxes on hunting and fishing equipment, gas guzzler automobiles, vaccines, tires, and coal.[101] HCERA imposed two main excise taxes, the medical device excise tax[102] and, beginning in 2018, a forty percent excise tax on the value of health insurance benefits exceeding a certain threshold.[103]

These excise taxes were added to the list of excise taxes that already existed under subtitle D of the Internal Revenue Code.[104] The origins of several of the excise taxes that have been confused for originating in HCERA are summarized in *Table 1*.

Table 1. The Origins of Select Excise Taxes

Subject of the Excise Tax	Originating Act
Sporting equipment	Excise Tax Reduction Act of 1965 – Section 205
Gas guzzler automobiles	Energy Tax Act of 1978 – Section 201
Vaccines	Vaccine Compensation Amendments of 1987 – Section 9201
Tires	Highway Revenue Act of 1956 – Section 204(a)
Coal	Black Lung Benefits Revenue Act of 1977 – Section 2(a)

Source: Created by CRS.

What Bills Have Been Introduced to Repeal the Medical Device Excise Tax?

Table 2 contains a list of major bills and resolutions in the 112th and 113th Congresses to fully repeal the medical device excise tax.

Table 2. Proposals to Repeal the Medical Device Excise Tax

Bill or Resolution Number	Title	Title	Last Action
H.R. 523—113th	Protect Medical Innovation Act of 2013	2/6/13	Referred to House Ways and Means
H.R. 1295—113th	Medical Device Tax Elimination Act	3/20/13	Referred to House Ways and Means
H.J.Res. 59 EAH—113th	Resolved, That the House agree to the amendment of the Senate to the resolution (H.J.Res. 59) entitled `Joint Resolution making continuing appropriations for fiscal year 2014, and for other purposes.', with the following	9/29/13	In conference
S. 232—113th	Medical Device Access and Innovation Protection Act	2/7/13	Referred to Senate Finance
S.J.Res. 8—113th	A joint resolution providing for congressional disapproval under chapter 8 of title 5, United States Code, of the rule submitted by the Internal Revenue Service of the Department of the Treasury relating to taxable medical devices.	2/27/13	Referred to Senate Finance
S.Amdt. 297 to S.Con.Res. 8—113th	To promote innovation, preserve high-paying jobs, and encourage economic growth for manufacturers of lifesaving medical devices and cutting edge medical therapies	3/21/13	Agreed to on a 79-20 vote; Held at the desk 4/15/13
H.R. 436—112th	Health Care Cost Reduction Act of 2012	1/25/11	Passed House, 270-146, Placed on Senate Legislative Calendar 6/12/12
H.R. 488—112th	Save Our Medical Devices Act of 2011	1/26/11	Referred to House Ways and

Bill or Resolution Number	Title	Title	Last Action
			Means
H.R. 734—112th	To amend the Internal Revenue Code of 1986 to repeal the medical device tax, and for other purposes	2/16/11	Referred to House Ways and Means & Appropriations
H.R. 1310—112th	To amend the Internal Revenue Code of 1986 to exempt certain emergency medical devices from the excise tax on medical devices, and for other purposes.	4/1/11	Referred to House Ways and Means
H.R. 4064—112th	Keeping Promises to Taxpayers Act of 2012	2/16/12	Referred to House Ways and Means & Energy and Commerce
H.R. 5906—112th	To amend the Internal Revenue Code of 1986 to repeal the excise tax on medical devices	6/7/12	Referred to House Ways and Means
H.R. 6088—112th	Total Repeal of the Unfair Taxes on Healthcare Act of 2012	7/9/12	Referred to House Subcommittee on Health
H.Res. 679—112th	Providing for consideration of the bill (H.R. 436) to amend the Internal Revenue Code of 1986 to repeal the excise tax on medical devices, and providing for consideration of the bill (H.R. 5882) making appropriations for the Legislative Branch for the fiscal year ending September 30, 2013, and for other purposes.	6/6/12	Agreed to in House, 241-173, 6/7/12
S. 17—112th	Medical Device Access and Innovation Protection Act	1/25/11	Referred to Senate Finance
S. 262—112th	A bill to repeal the excise tax on medical device manufacturers.	2/3/11	Referred to Senate Finance
S.J.Res. 51—112th	A joint resolution providing for congressional disapproval under chapter 8 of title 5, United States Code, of the rule submitted by the Internal Revenue Service of the Department of the Treasury relating to taxable medical devices.	12/21/12	Referred to Senate Finance

Source: Created by CRS.

End Notes

[1] The medical device excise tax was included in an amended version of the Affordable Care Act. See Health Care and Education Reconciliation Act of 2010, P.L. 111-152, Title I, Subtitle E, §1405(a)(1), 124 Stat. 1029, (2010) (amending the Patient Protection and Affordable Care Act of 2010, P.L. 111-148).

[2] See I.R.C. §4191(a). The medical device excise tax is only one of several provisions created under the HCERA or Patient Protection and Affordable Care Act to raise revenues to pay for expanded health insurance coverage. See CRS Report R41128, Health-Related Revenue Provisions in the Patient Protection and Affordable Care Act (ACA), by Janemarie Mulvey.

[3] See supra footnote 1, §1405(c). For medical devices financed through an installment sale or a long-term lease, the regulations do not provide any relief for payments made for a device after December 31, 2012, unless that agreement was entered into prior to March 30, 2010, the date the ACA was enacted. See Treas. Reg. §48.4191-1(f) (citing Treas. Reg. §48.4216(c)-1(e)).

[4] See Letter to the Honorable Harry Reid from 18 Current and Future Members of the Senate, (December 4, 2012) http://www.franken.senate.gov/?p=hot_topic&id=2248.

[5] A bill repealing the medical device excise tax passed the House of Representatives in the 112th Congress. See Health Care Cost Reduction Act of 2012, H.R. 436 (2012). Other similar bills have been presented in the 113th Congress. See Protect Medical Innovation Act of 2013, H.R. 523 (2013); see also Medical Device Tax Elimination Act, H.R. 1295 (2013); Medical Device Access and Innovation Protection Act, S. 232 (2013); A joint resolution providing for congressional disapproval under chapter 8 of title 5, United States Code, of the rule submitted by the Internal Revenue Service of the Department of the Treasury relating to taxable medical devices, S.J.Res. 8 (2013).

[6] See, e.g., Melissa Attias and Emily Ethridge, Medicare Board, Device Tax Lead House GOP Target List, Roll Call, January 22, 2013, http://www.cq.com/doc/news-4208077?wr =eFF6UlQqRXM3azJhbDBGWEpQWjBIUQ.

[7] See "Taxable Medical Devices," 77 Fed. Reg. 72,924 (December 7, 2012).

[8] This report does not discuss the general Treasury regulations for manufacturer excise taxes unless those regulations uniquely impact the medical device excise tax.

[9] For explanation of the definition of the "price" of an article taxed under Chapter 32 of the Internal Revenue Code, see I.R.C. §4216(a).

[10] See I.R.C. §4191(a).

[11] See 77 Fed. Reg. at 72930. Notably, the general exemptions for excise taxes provided to manufacturers who sell an article to a state or local government or to a nonprofit educational organization do not apply to the medical device excise tax. See I.R.C. §4221(a).

[12] See Treas. Reg. §48.0-2(4)(i). The general definitions for a manufacturer, producer, and importer are incorporated by reference into the regulations clarifying the medical device excise tax. See Treas. Reg. §48.4191-1(c). The Internal Revenue Code does not subject a manufacturer to an excise tax if the sale of the article is for use by the purchaser for further manufacturing. See I.R.C. §4221(a)(1).

[13] Id. Treasury regulations also explain that the term "importer," while typically entailing the person who brings an "article into the United States from a source outside the United States," can also include the beneficial owner of an item if, for example, a customs broker is engaged by an entity to bring a particular item into the country. Id. In contrast, the Internal Revenue Code exempts a manufacturer from being subject to an excise tax when the sale of the article is for export. See I.R.C. §4221(a)(2).

[14] See Ruan Financial Corp. v. United States, 765 F. Supp. 987-88 (S.D. Iowa 1990), aff'd 976 F.2d 452 (8th Cir. 1992).

[15] I.R.C. §4191(a).

[16] Id. at (b)(1) (citing 21 U.S.C. §321(h)).

[17] See Committee of Dental Amalgam Mfrs. & Distribs. v. Stratton, 92 F.3d 807, 810 (9th Cir. 1996); see also United States v. McGuff, 781 F. Supp. 654, 655 (C.D. Cal. 1991).

[18] 21 C.F.R. §880.6230.

[19] 21 C.F.R. Part 870, subpart D.

[20] Specifically, the Food, Drug, and Cosmetics Act defines a medical device as an "instrument, apparatus, implement, machine, contrivance, implant, in vitro reagent, or other similar or related article including any component, parts or accessory which is" either (1) "recognized in the official National Formulary, or the United States Pharmacopeia, or any supplement to them," (2) "intended for use in the diagnosis of disease or other conditions, or in the cure, mitigation, treatment, or prevention of disease, or other animals," or (3) "intended to affect the structure or any function of the body of man or other animals, and which does not achieve its primary intended purposes through chemical action within or on the body of man or other animals and which is not dependent upon being metabolized for the achievement of its primary intended purposes." See 21 U.S.C. §321(h).

[21] 21 U.S.C. §360(j).

[22] For a general explanation of the medical device regulatory framework, see CRS Report R42130, FDA Regulation of Medical Devices, by Judith A. Johnson. Devices used exclusively in veterinary medicine are not listed under Section 510(j) of the FFDCA and 21 CFR Part 807, and, therefore, Treasury's regulations are exclusive to devices that are intended, at least in part, for use on humans.

[23] 77 Fed. Reg. at 72,925-26. However, medical kits created by a hospital or medical institution are exempt from the excise tax, as the creations of such kits are necessarily excluded from the FDA's registration and listing requirements. See 21 C.F.R. §807.65(f).

[24] See Food and Drug Administration, How FDA Regulates Veterinary Devices, (January 20, 2012), http://www.fda.gov/AnimalVeterinary/ResourcesforYou/ucm047117.htm.

[25] 21 C.F.R. §880.6250.

[26] I.R.C. §4191(b)(2).

[27] Id. §4191(b)(2)(A)-(C).

[28] Id. §4191(b)(2)(D); see also Joint Committee on Taxation, General Explanation of Tax Legislation Enacted in the 111th Congress, committee print, prepared by Staff of the Joint Committee on Taxation, 111th Cong., March 2011, JCS-2-11, p. 366 ("The Secretary may determine that a specific medical device is exempt under the provision if the device is generally sold at retail establishments (including over the internet) to individuals for their personal use.")

[29] Treas. Reg. §48.4191-2(b)(2).

[30] Id.

[31] Id.

[32] Id.

[33] For more detail on the factors implicating whether a device can be considered regularly available for purchase and use by individual consumers, see Treas. Reg. §48.4191-2(b)(2)(i)(A)-(C). With respect to devices classified by the FDA as a "physical medicine device," such devices are listed under subpart D of 21 CFR part 890, and include devices such as canes, see 21 C.F.R. §890.3075, crutches, id. §890.3150, and wheelchairs, id. §§890.3850 - 890.3860.

[34] See Treas. Reg. §48.4191-2(b)(2)(iv)(Example 2).

[35] Id.

[36] See Treas. Reg. §48.4191-2(b)(2)(ii)(A)-(E).

[37] The regulations specifically cite as a factor a devices' classification as a Class III device, the medical devices subject to the most intensive pre-market screening by the FDA, see CRS Report R42130, FDA Regulation of Medical Devices, by Judith A. Johnson, to be relevant in determining whether a device should be subject to the retail exemption. See Treas. Reg. §48.4191-2(b)(2)(ii)(C). In addition, the new Treasury regulations explain that the FDA's classification of a device under one of fifteen various categories of medical devices in the Code of Federal Regulations is an additional factor to examine when determining whether to apply the retail exemption. Id. §48.4191-2(b)(2)(ii)(D).

[38] See Treas. Reg. §48.4191-2(b)(2)(ii)(D) (citing 42 C.F.R. part 210).

[39] See Treas. Reg. §48.4191-2(b)(2)(iv)(Example 2).

[40] Id.

[41] Id.

[42] 77 Fed. Reg. at 72,929.

[43] See Treas. Reg. §48.4191-2(b)(iii).

[44] Id. at 72927.

[45] See Treas. Reg. §48.4191-2(b)(2)(iii)(A)-(C).

[46] Id. §48.4191-2(b)(2)(iii)(D).

[47] Id. §48.4191-2(b)(2)(iii)(D)(4).

[48] Id. §48.4191-2(b)(2)(iv).

[49] Id. (Example 2).

[50] Id. (Example 7).

[51] Id. (Example 13).

[52] Id. (Example 1).

[53] Id. (Example 2).

[54] Id. (Example 3).

[55] Id. (Example 4).

[56] Id. (Example 9).

[57] Id. (Example 10).

[58] Id. (Example 14).

[59] Id. (Example 6).

[60] Id. (Example 7).

[61] Id. (Example 8).

[62] Id. (Example 11).

[63] Id. (Example 5).

[64] Id. (Example 12).

[65] Id. (Example 13).

[66] Id. (Example 15).

[67] See supra footnote 4.

[68] See Treas. Reg. § 48.4191-2(b)(2)(iii)(A)-(C).

[69] Several of the factors used to determine the scope of the retail exemption are FDA regulations relating to safety controls on the release of medical devices or Medicare Part B payment rules. See, e.g., Treas. Reg. §§48.4191-2(i)(C), (ii)(C)-(E).

[70] 77 Fed. Reg. at 72931.

[71] Id. at 72932.

[72] See supra note footnote 22.

[73] 77 Fed. Reg. at 72933.

[74] See supra footnote 5.

[75] See "To promote innovation, preserve high-paying jobs, and encourage economic growth for manufacturers of lifesaving medical devices and cutting edge medical therapies," S.Amdt. 297 to S.Con.Res. 8 (2013).

[76] See Office of Management and Budget, "Statement of Administration Policy," June 6, 2012, http://www.whitehouse.gov/sites/default/files/omb/legislative/sap/112/saphr436r_20120606 .pdf ("If the President were presented with H.R. 436, his senior advisors would recommend that he veto the bill.").

[77] See Honorable Harry Reid, "Reid Statement on Latest Republican Attempt to Force a Government Shutdown," September 30, 2013, http://www.reid.senate.gov/reid_statement_ on_latest_republican_ attempt_to_force_a_government_shutdown.cfm ("To be absolutely clear, the Senate will reject both the one-year delay of the Affordable Care Act and the repeal of the medical device tax.")

[78] I.R.C. §4191.

[79] I.R.C. §4191(a).

[80] See Health Care and Education Reconciliation Act of 2010, P.L. 111-152, Title I, Subtitle E, § 1405(d) ("EFFECTIVE DATE. – The amendments made by this section shall apply to sales after December 31, 2012).

[81] See Treas. Reg. §48.4191-1(f).

[82] See Health Care and Education Reconciliation Act of 2010, P.L. 111-152, Title I, Subtitle E, § 1405(b)

[83] See 31 U.S.C. § 3302(b).

[84] Id.

[85] See Securities and Exchange Commission—Reduction of Obligation of Appropriated Funds Due to Sublease (7/19/96) Comp. Gen. Dec. No. B-265727.

[86] See I.R.C. § 4191(b).

[87] See Treas. Reg. §48.4191-2(a).

[88] See supra "What is a 'Taxable Medical Device'"

[89] See I.R.C. §4191(b).

[90] Id.

[91] See Treas. Reg. § 48.4191-2 (examples).

[92] Id.

[93] See supra "The Retail Exemption's Safe Harbor Provisions"

[94] See Treas. Reg. § 40.6011(a)-1.

[95] See Treas. Reg. § 40.6302(c)-1(a). Entities with tax liability of $2,500 or less need not file the semimonthly deposit. Id. § 40.6302(c)-1(f).

[96] See I.R.C. § 6656.

[97] See Internal Revenue Service, "Interim Guidance and Request for Comments; Medical Device Excise Tax; Manufacturers Excise Taxes; Constructive Sale Price; Deposit Penalties," Notice 2012-77, Section 6, http://www.irs.gov/pub/irs-drop/n-12-77.pdf ("In consideration of the short time frame between the effective date of the tax and the due date of the first deposit, and in the interest of sound tax administration, the IRS and the Treasury Department have decided to provide temporary relief from the § 6656 penalty for the first three calendar quarters of 2013.").

[98] See I.R.C. § 4191(b).

[99] See, e.g., PoliFact, "A hidden provision in Obamacare taxes sporting goods as medical devices," June 12, 2013, www.politifact.com/ohio/statements/2013/jun/14/chain-email/chain-email-claims-health-care-law-contains-hidden/.

[100] See "Cabela's blames 'glitch' for Jan. 1 tax error, promises refunds," Omaha World-Herald, January 8, 2013, http://omaha.com/article/20130108/MONEY/701089985/1101.

[101] See FactCheck.org, "Cabela's Medical Tax Mistake," September 18, 2013, http://www.factcheck.org/2013/09/ cabelas-medical-tax-mistake/.

[102] See Health Care and Education Reconciliation Act of 2010, P.L. 111-152, Title I, Subtitle E, § 1405.

[103] Id. § 1401.

[104] See I.R.C. §§ 4001 et seq.

In: The Medical Device Excise Tax
Editor: Nina Kimball-Veronesi

ISBN: 978-1-63117-598-5
© 2014 Nova Science Publishers, Inc.

Chapter 3

MEDICAL DEVICE EXCISE TAX: FREQUENTLY ASKED QUESTIONS*

Internal Revenue Service

Q1. What is the medical device excise tax?

A1. Section 4191 of the Internal Revenue Code imposes an excise tax on the sale of certain medical devices by the manufacturer or importer of the device.

Q2. When does the tax go into effect?

A2. The tax applies to sales of taxable medical devices after Dec. 31, 2012.

Q3. How much is the tax?

A3. The tax is 2.3 percent of the sale price of the taxable medical device. See Chapter 5 of IRS Publication 510, Excise Taxes, and Notice 2012-77 for additional information on the determination of sale price.

Q4. Who is responsible for reporting and paying the medical device excise tax?

A4. Generally, the manufacturer or importer of a taxable medical device is responsible for filing Form 720, Quarterly Federal Excise Tax Return, and paying the tax to the IRS.

Q5. Will individual consumers be subject to any reporting or recordkeeping requirements?

---

* This is an edited, reformatted and augmented version of the following IRS website, http:// www.irs.gov/uac/Medical-Device-Excise-Tax:-Frequently-Asked-Questions,viewed January 2014.

A5. Generally, no action is required by individual consumers. Because the tax is imposed upon the sale of a taxable medical device by the manufacturer or importer, the manufacturer or importer is responsible for reporting and paying the tax.

Q6. Who is the manufacturer for purposes of the medical device excise tax?

A6. Generally, with regard to the medical device excise tax, the manufacturer is the person who produces a taxable medical device from scrap, salvage or junk material, or from new or raw material, by processing, manipulating or changing the form of a device or by combining or assembling two or more devices.

Q7. Who is the importer for purposes of the medical device excise tax?

A7. Generally, with regard to the medical device excise tax, the importer of a taxable medical device is the person who brings the device into the United States from a source outside the United States, or withdraws the device from a customs-bonded warehouse for sale or use in the United States.

Q8. What is the tax treatment of convenience kits?

A8. Notice 2012-77 provides interim guidance on the tax treatment of convenience kits. Under the interim guidance, a taxable medical device that goes into a domestically-produced convenience kit will be subject to tax upon its sale by the manufacturer or importer, but the sale of the convenience kit by the kit producer will not be subject to tax. Special rules apply to imported kits.

For purposes of the notice, a convenience kit is a set of two or more devices within the meaning of § 201(h) of the Federal Food, Drug, and Cosmetic Act that is enclosed in a single package, such as a bag, tray, or box, for the convenience of a health care professional or the end user.

Q9. What form will be used to report the medical device excise tax?

A9. The medical device excise tax is a manufacturers excise tax. Like other manufacturers excise taxes, the medical device excise tax is reported on Form 720. See Chapters 11 and 12 of IRS Publication 510 for additional information on filing, deposits, and payments.

Q10. When is the Form 720 due?

A10. Form 720 is filed quarterly. The first return to report the medical device excise tax will be due on April 30, 2013, for the quarterly period including January, February and March 2013. Quarterly return due dates are as follows:

For the months:	Due by:
Jan., Feb., Mar.	April 30
Apr., May, Jun.	July 31
Jul., Aug., Sep.	Oct. 31
Oct., Nov., Dec.	Jan. 31

Q11. Are tax deposits required for the medical device excise tax?

A11. Yes. Semi-monthly deposits will generally be required if tax liability exceeds $2,500 for the quarter. The first deposit of the medical device excise tax, covering the first 15 days of January 2013, will be due on Jan. 29, 2013. Notice 2012-77 provides transition relief from deposit penalties during the first three calendar quarters of 2013. For details on deposit requirements, see the Instructions to Form 720 and Chapter 12 of IRS Publication 510.

Q12. Should an entity that is disregarded for income tax purposes file Form 720 in the disregarded entity's name or the owner's name?

A12. An entity that is disregarded as an entity separate from its owner for income tax purposes is treated as a separate entity for excise tax purposes. Therefore, the entity, and not the disregarded entity's owner, is responsible for filing Form 720 and paying of the tax.

Q13. Has the IRS issued guidance on the medical device excise tax?

A13. Yes. The IRS and the Treasury Department issued final regulations on Dec. 5, 2012. The IRS and the Treasury Department issued Notice 2012-77 on Dec. 5, 2012, to provide interim guidance on certain issues related to the medical device excise tax.

Q14. What is a taxable medical device?

A14. In general, a taxable medical device is a device that is listed as a device with the Food and Drug Administration under section 510(j) of the Federal Food, Drug, and Cosmetic Act and 21 CFR part 807, unless the device falls within an exemption from the tax, such as the retail exemption.

Q15. Are there any exemptions to the medical device excise tax?

A15. Yes. There are specific statutory exemptions for eyeglasses, contact lenses, and hearing aids. There is also an exemption for other devices that are of a type that are generally purchased by the general public at retail for individual use (the retail exemption).

Q16. How does a manufacturer determine if a particular type of device qualifies for the retail exemption?

A16. The regulations provide a facts and circumstances approach to determine whether a type of device meets the retail exemption. The regulations enumerate several factors that are relevant, but there may be relevant factors in addition to those enumerated in the regulations. The determination is based on the overall balance of factors relevant to a particular type of device. No one factor is determinative. See § 48.4191-2(b)(2) of the regulations for more information about the retail exemption. The regulations also provide a safe harbor for certain devices that will be considered to be of a type that falls within the retail exemption. See Q&A 18.

Q17. Do the regulations illustrate how the retail exemption facts and circumstances test should be applied?

A17. Yes. The regulations include examples that apply the facts and circumstances test to several types of medical devices. Based on the totality of the circumstances presented in the examples, the examples conclude that non-sterile absorbent tipped applicators, adhesive bandages, snake bite suction kits, denture adhesives, mechanical and powered wheelchairs, portable oxygen concentrators, and therapeutic AC powered adjustable home use beds are devices that fall within the retail exemption. Based on the totality of the circumstances presented in the examples, the examples also conclude that mobile x-ray systems, nonabsorbable silk sutures, and nuclear magnetic resonance imaging systems are not devices that fall within the retail exemption.

Q18. Is there a retail exemption safe harbor?

A18. Yes. The regulations identify certain categories of devices that qualify for the retail exemption so that manufacturers and importers do not have to apply the facts and circumstances test. Those categories are set forth in a safe harbor provision in § 48.4191-2(b)(2)(iii) of the regulations.

Q19. Are there any circumstances under which a taxable medical device can be sold tax-free?

A19. Yes. A manufacturer or importer of a taxable medical device may, in certain circumstances, sell a taxable medical device tax-free for use by the purchaser for further manufacture (or for resale by the purchaser to a second purchaser for further manufacture), or for export (or for resale for export). To make a tax-free sale for further manufacture or export, both parties to the sale must be registered with the IRS. Form 637, Application for Registration for Certain Excise Tax Activities, is used for the registration process. For more information on the Form 637 registration process, see the 637 Registration Program at IRS.gov.

Q20. I'm not familiar with manufacturers excise taxes. Where can I learn more?

A20. For more information about manufacturers excise taxes in general, see Chapter 5 of IRS Publication 510.

In: The Medical Device Excise Tax
Editor: Nina Kimball-Veronesi

ISBN: 978-1-63117-598-5
© 2014 Nova Science Publishers, Inc.

Chapter 4

FEDERAL EXCISE TAXES: AN INTRODUCTION AND GENERAL ANALYSIS*

Sean Lowry

SUMMARY

There are four common types of excise taxes: (1) sumptuary (or "sin") taxes, (2) regulatory or environmental taxes, (3) benefit-based taxes (or user charges), and (4) luxury taxes. Sumptuary taxes were traditionally imposed for moral reasons, but are currently rationalized, in part, to discourage a specific activity that is thought to have negative spillover effects (or "externalities") on society. Regulatory or environmental taxes are imposed to offset external costs associated with regulating public safety or to discourage consumption of a specific commodity that is thought to have negative externalities on society. Benefit-based taxes (which include user charges) are imposed to charge users of a particular public good for financing and maintenance of that public good. Lastly, luxury taxes are primarily imposed as one way to raise revenue, particularly from higher-income households.

This report provides an introduction and general analysis of excise taxes. First, a brief history of U.S. excise tax policy is provided. Second, the various forms of excise taxes and their respective administrative

---

* This is an edited, reformatted and augmented version of Congressional Research Service, Publication No. R43189, dated August 26, 2013.

advantages and disadvantages are described. Third, the effect of federal excise taxes on federal, state, and local tax revenue is discussed. Fourth, the economic effects of various types of excise taxes are analyzed. The effects on consumer behavior and equity among taxpayers could be important issues for assessment of current excise tax policy or for the design of new excise taxes.

Excise taxes have generally played a diminishing role in financing the federal government since the middle of the 20th century for multiple reasons. First, Congress has taken legislative action to eliminate many categories of excise taxes. Second, most excise tax rates set in statute have declined in value over time due to inflation and inaction by Congress to change tax rates set in statute.

Excise taxes tend to be regressive, in that lower-income households generally pay a larger share of their income in excise taxes than higher-income households. Because excise taxes generally increase the price of the taxed commodity, they also tend to lower consumer demand.

Excise taxes play a much smaller role in financing the federal government than they did in the past. In 1960, federal excise tax collections were $355.49 billion (in 2012 constant dollars, after accounting for inflation). In FY2012, federal excise tax collections were $56.17 billion (roughly one-sixth of their 1960 value in 2012 constant dollars). Federal excise taxes comprised 7.0% of all federal revenue in 1973, whereas they comprised 3.2% in 2012.

Congress may be interested in revisiting the revenue and economic effects of excise taxes because these taxes could play a growing role in financing public goods. Some long-standing excise tax proposals to correct alleged social costs have resurfaced from time to time in policy discussions. Some of these proposals could be targeted towards specific products or activities (e.g., a "sugar-sweetened beverages" tax), while others could affect a broad range of economic activity and raise a significant amount of revenue (e.g., a carbon tax). On the other hand, there is also interest in reducing current excise tax rates as a means to encourage short-term growth in particular industries.

INTRODUCTION

Excise taxes are selective taxes on specific forms of consumption or behavior (compared to general sales taxes which tend to apply to all forms of consumption, with some exceptions). Today, federal excise taxes apply to a wide variety of consumer goods and economic activities, such as alcohol, tobacco, firearms and ammunition, gasoline, the industrial use of ozone-depleting chemicals, and indoor tanning services.

There are four common purposes of excise taxes: (1) sumptuary (or "sin") taxes, (2) regulatory or environmental taxes, (3) benefit-based taxes (or user charges), and (4) luxury taxes.[1] Sumptuary (or "sin") taxes were traditionally imposed for moral reasons, but are currently rationalized, in part, to discourage a specific activity that is thought to have negative spillover effects (or "externalities") on society.[2] Generally, sumptuary taxes in the United States refer to excise taxes on alcohol or tobacco consumption. Regulatory or environmental taxes are imposed to offset for external costs associated with regulating public safety or to discourage consumption of a specific commodity that is thought to have negative externalities on society. Benefit-based taxes are imposed to charge users for the benefits received from a particular public good and are often used for maintenance and upkeep of that public good. Lastly, luxury taxes are primarily imposed as one way to raise revenue, particularly from higher-income households.[3]

The role of excise taxes has changed over time. Excise taxes narrowly imposed on the consumption of certain products, such as alcohol and tobacco, formed the basis for much of federal tax revenue until the modern income tax was enacted in the early 20th century. Although excise taxes have played a diminishing role in the mix of federal revenue sources over time, there has been persistent interest in the possible use of excise taxes to raise revenue or provide disincentives to behavior that is believed by some to have negative effects on society (e.g., a tax on carbon emissions). On the other hand, there is also interest in reducing current excise tax rates as a means to encourage short-term growth in particular industries.[4]

This report provides an introduction and general analysis of excise taxes. First, a brief history of the role of excise taxes is provided.

Second, the various forms of excise taxes and their respective administrative advantages and disadvantages are described.

Third, the effect of federal excise taxes on federal, state, and local tax revenue is discussed. Fourth, the economic effects of various types of excise taxes are analyzed. The effects on consumer behavior and equity among taxpayers could be important issues for assessment of current excise tax policy or for the design of new excise taxes.

Lastly, the **Appendix** to this report contains a list of references to other CRS reports on specific excise taxes.[5]

HISTORICAL SUMMARY OF FEDERAL EXCISE TAXES

Federal excise taxes have had a dynamic role within the U.S. tax system. The history of the federal excise tax system is often one that coincides with wars, serving as an emergency source of funds, or reflects periodic concerns about rising budget deficits.[6] Except for taxes on tobacco and liquor, new excise taxes seem to have been used extensively for the control of social costs and as user charges in recent years.

Excise taxes played a key fiscal role in the early history of the United States.[7] The federal government initially relied on customs duties (tariffs) on foreign trade. In 1791, during the presidency of George Washington, Secretary of the Treasury Alexander Hamilton implemented the first federal excise tax on whiskey. The whiskey tax was used as a means to fund the fledgling federal government, repay debts from the American Revolution, and help to establish federal supremacy over the states.[8] The burden of the tax was controversial along geographic divisions (Westerners on the frontier tended to both consume more whiskey and use it as a medium of financial exchange) and ideological divisions (Federalists versus Anti-Federalists). This opposition peaked in the famous "Whiskey Rebellion" of 1794 in southwestern Pennsylvania, where President Washington led 13,000 troops to suppress an armed rebellion. After the suppression of the Whiskey Rebellion in 1794, Congress passed excise taxes on tobacco, snuff tobacco, sugar, and carriages.[9] In 1797, a direct tax was imposed on the ownership of houses, land, and slaves as tariff revenue declined during a period when European powers were engaged in war (with the United States sided against France). The unpopularity of the taxes contributed to Thomas Jefferson's defeat of Federalist Party candidate John Adams during the presidential election of 1800. All internal excise taxes were repealed in 1802, as the fiscal demand arising from the war in Europe abated.[10]

Federal excise taxes continued to play a significant role in public finances throughout the 1800s. Excises were temporarily reintroduced during the War of 1812, but were repealed from 1817 until the Civil War.[11] Following the onset of the Civil War, Congress passed the Revenue Act of 1861, which restored earlier excise taxes.[12] Most of these excise taxes were repealed after the end of the Civil War, with taxes on distilled spirits and tobacco remaining in effect. In the decades after the Civil War, excise taxes accounted for between one-third and one-half of all federal revenue.[13] Excises were the single largest source of internal revenue during this era.[14] During the Spanish-American War (1898), excise tax revenue was a larger source of federal tax collections than even customs duties on foreign imports, as revenue from tariffs tended to decline during wartime. Emergency excise taxes were levied on a variety of items to fund military spending during the Spanish-American War, such as pianos, playing cards, yachts, and billiard tables. After the end of the war most of these emergency excise taxes were repealed.

Excise taxes were utilized to fund war-time spending during the early 20th century. Temporary excise tax provisions were imposed in the Revenue Act of 1918, passed during World War I, to help fund war-time spending, including the first excise tax on firearms, shells, and cartridges. As a result, excise tax collections quadrupled from 1914 to 1919.[15] Excise tax revenues declined significantly after the beginning of Prohibition (falling to less than half of the pre-Prohibition revenue levels by 1930) but rebounded above the pre-Prohibition levels after the consumption of alcohol was made legal again after 1933.[16] Existing excise tax rates were increased again virtually across-the-board around the time of World War II, and new taxes on luxury goods (such as toiletries and furs) were introduced.[17] Additionally, Congress rejected adopting a general sales tax twice during this era (1932 and 1942), despite critiques that the costs of administering excises to a growing list of products was high and the revenue gained from many excises was small.[18]

Excise taxes underwent a time of dynamic reform during the latter half of the 20th century. The Revenue Act of 1951 increased many excise tax rates in existence at the time (such as alcohol and tobacco) and increased the tax base for some user charges. However, the Excise Tax Reduction Act of 1954 (P.L. 83-324) and the Excise Tax Reduction Act of 1965 (P.L. 89-44) reduced the number of provisions and their respective tax rates. In particular, the Excise Tax Reduction Act of 1965 eliminated most federal excise taxes with the goal being to "help sustain economic expansion."[19]

Certain excise taxes were also expanded, in part, to reflect a desire for a wider role for the federal government. An example of this linkage between excise taxes and the expansion of federally provided public goods would be the modern highway system.[20] The Highway Revenue Act of 1956 (P.L. 84-627) increased the federal gasoline tax (in effect since 1932) and directed its collections from the Treasury's General Fund specifically towards funding of public highways.[21] Specific excise taxes linked to trust funds related to air travel, mining, waterway travel, oil spills, and other hazardous chemicals (among others) were created in the 1970s and 1980s. A rising budget deficit helped to bring about the excise tax increases in the Omnibus Budget Reconciliation Act of 1990 (OBRA90; P.L. 101-508). OBRA90 increased tax rates on distilled spirits (last increased in 1985), beer and wine (last increased in 1951), tobacco (last increased in 1982), and gasoline (last increased in 1982).

Since 2000, excise taxes have played a diminishing role in the mix of federal revenue sources even as new provisions have been introduced. As discussed later in the "Revenue" section of this report, excise tax collections have increased in nominal amounts, but have decreased in inflation-adjusted (real) values and as a share of overall federal revenue. The rates on major excise taxes have remained unadjusted for inflation for years, such as the excise taxes on gasoline (since 1997) and alcohol (1991). The excise tax on tobacco was last increased with the Children's Health Insurance Program Reauthorization Act of 2009 (P.L. 111-3), but revenue from the tobacco tax has declined over time in part due to decreased demand for tobacco products.

Recently, new excise taxes have been introduced. Several new excise taxes were created by the Patient Protection and Affordable Care Act (P.L. 111-148 and P.L. 111-152, as amended), such as taxes on indoor tanning bed services, medical devices, and certain high-value insurance plans.

The future role of federal excise taxes in federal policy is still unclear. Excise taxes in the form of user charges could continue to play a role in financing public goods and services. Excises could be one tool to raise revenue, particularly in the absence of a general consumption tax at the federal level.[22] Some long-standing excise tax proposals to correct a perceived social issue have also resurfaced in policy discussions. Some of these proposals could be targeted towards specific products or activities (e.g., a "sugar-sweetened beverages" tax), while others could affect a broad range of economic activity and raise a significant amount of revenue (e.g., a carbon tax).[23]

ADMINISTRATION

All forms of excise tax use some sort of physical control or measurement by the excise authorities to determine tax liability and ensure compliance with the law.[24] This section of the report describes the different ways that excise taxes are structured, and the advantages and disadvantages of each model.

Setting the Tax Rate

For excise taxes intended to compensate for the social costs of certain activities, economic theory suggests that the excise tax rate should be set at a level that offsets the negative costs of that consumption to society.[25]

In general, an excise tax rate can be applied in one of two ways:

- *Per unit*: where the tax rate is applied per individual unit produced, purchased, or sold. For example, different per-unit rates are levied on tobacco products based on the product type: 1,000 units of cigarettes or one pound of pipe tobacco.
- *Ad valorem*: where the tax rate is applied as a percentage of the value of the product, either based on the manufacturer's, wholesale, or retail price. For example, the excise tax on firearms and ammunition is set at 10% of the wholesale price for pistols and revolvers, and 11% for other firearms as well as shells or cartridges.[26]

Economists say that per-unit excise taxes are more appropriate when marginal consumption of the targeted commodity is allegedly deleterious. For example, cigarette taxes are levied per unit sold because the alleged spillover effects of smoking (e.g., second-hand smoking) occur with every pack of cigarettes smoked. The excise tax on gasoline is levied per gallon of gasoline sold because the amount of gasoline consumed was a rough approximation of how much driving one did, and thus how much wear and tear a driver would impose on federally managed highways.

However, arguments can be made against these justifications for per unit taxes. Per-unit taxes can invite issues of both horizontal and vertical equality (as addressed later in this report). Also, because per-unit taxes are often set at static rates in statute, these rates often fall in inflation-adjusted (or "real") terms.[27] For example, the statutory federal excise tax rate on distilled spirits in 1951 was set to $10.50 per proof gallon (ppg).[28] Legislation was passed in 1985 increasing the statutory tax rate from $10.50 to $12.50 ppg, and again in 1990 increasing the tax rate from $12.50 to $13.50 ppg. The excise tax rate on distilled spirits still remains at the 1990 level of $13.50 ppg, or $2.14 per 750ml bottle (a "fifth") of 80-proof liquor.[29] If the 1951 tax rate was indexed for inflation, it would be over $95.65 ppg in 2013 dollars, or approximately $19.49 per 750 ml bottle of 80 proof liquor.[30]

In contrast, *ad valorem* tax rates largely avoid a real decline in value because they are applied based on the price of commodity or activity rather than the quantity consumed or produced. *Ad valorem* rates can also be more progressive than per-unit rates especially if the commodity taxed is a luxury good (whereby demand increases more than proportionally as income rises). However, *ad valorem* rates also have the capability to be regressive if the consumers of the commodity are not limited to those at the upper end of the income distribution.

Choosing the Stage of Production to Levy the Tax

An excise tax can also be levied at different stages along a commodity's production and distribution chain:[31]

- Production level: collected on sales by producers to wholesalers, retailers, or other producers. Transactions prior to the sale by the last producer are often partially exempted or taxed at reduced rates.
- Manufacturing level: collected on sales by manufacturers to wholesalers or retailers, including occasional direct sales to consumers.
- Wholesale level: collected on sales by the last wholesaler or manufacturer to retailers, including occasional direct sales to consumers.
- Retail level: collected on sales by retailers to final consumer, including wholesalers or manufacturers selling occasionally to consumers.
- Turnover taxes: collected on sales at all or nearly all stages, and also known as "cascade taxes" on account of their cumulative effects.

Generally, an excise tax that is levied at earlier stages in the production process has lower administrative costs and fewer opportunities for tax evasion. In most situations, consumers vastly outnumber producers. Trying to implement an excise tax at the level of the consumer retail outlet results often in a duplication of bureaucratic processes compared to a tax on manufacturers. For example, more than 303 billion cigarettes were purchased across the United States in 2010, but 85% of these cigarettes were manufactured by three companies.[32] However, *ad valorem* taxes imposed at the manufacturer's level could provide an incentive for value-added options to be ordered further down the supply chain in an attempt to minimize the tax burden. For example, the manufacturer tax on firearms is levied on the assembly of a complete rifle, but any add-ons or modification kits to that rifle are not taxed.[33]

Taxes imposed at the manufacturing level could lead to an effective tax rate that is higher than the statutory tax rate. This outcome occurs because some manufactured goods have a long inventory life, and a considerable time period may elapse between when the tax is paid (when the good leaves the manufacturer's premises) and the date that the good is sold. In effect, the manufacturer incurs an interest cost to borrow the money to pay the tax.[34]

The advantage of imposing a tax at the retail level is that it can more easily exclude certain consumers from an excise tax's revenue base, if desired. For example, farmers can receive an excise tax credit for certain fuel purchased for farm use, as this activity generally has a minimal effect on the quality of interstate highways.[35] On the other hand, exemptions could diminish the effect of the tax on the original goal of the tax. An exemption, in the form of a refund, can be implemented through a manufacturer's tax, although this might require additional administrative resources.

Transition Issues

Special rules are sometimes used to accompany the imposition of a new excise tax or increases in any existing tax rates to prevent tax avoidance. If an excise tax is announced effective as of a specific date in the future, then individuals might stockpile the taxed commodity. One policy to prevent this behavior is a "floor stocks" tax, or an excise tax on all existing inventory as of a particular date. The floor stocks tax is usually imposed on the date a new tax takes effect or the date after a tax-rate increase takes effect; all new inventory subject to tax that is acquired after the new tax becomes effective is then subject to the new tax.

Excise Tax Reporting

Tax liability for most federal excise taxes is reported on IRS Form 720 "Quarterly Federal Excise Tax Return." This form is generally due at the end of April, July, October, and January, and reports taxes due the preceding quarter ending March, June, September, and December, respectively.[36] Most of the excise taxpayers using Form 720 must deposit the tax owed before filing the form with the IRS. Several excise taxes trigger a requirement to file a form in addition to Form 720 (e.g., Form 6197 [Gas Guzzler Tax], Form 2290 [Heavy Highway Vehicle Use Tax Return], and Form 6627 [Environmental Taxes]).

REVENUE

Excise taxes have had a diminishing role in federal public finance over time. Several forms of data analysis, presented in this section, illustrate this point.

One concern with per unit excise taxes is that they are often set in statute at specific levels, thus the inflation-adjusted value, or *real value*, often falls over time.[37] This trend usually continues absent legislative action to increase the statutory rates to reflect the effects of inflation.[38] The decline in the real value of excise tax receipts over time is apparent in Figure 1.

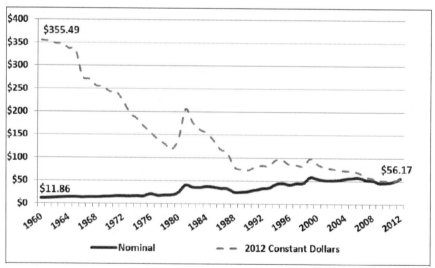

Source: CRS analysis of Internal Revenue Service, Table 6, *Databook*, 2012, at http://www.irs.gov/pub/irs-soi/ 12databk.pdf; and Office of Management and Budget, *Budget of the United States*, Historical Tables - Table 10.1, 2013, at http://www.whitehouse.gov/omb/budget/historicals.

Figure 1. Federal Excise Tax Collections, Nominal and Real Amounts, 1960 to 2012; Amounts are in billions of dollars.

Although nominal excise tax collections have increased from $11.86 billion in FY1960 to $56.17 billion in FY2012 (an increase of more than five times), real excise tax revenue has decreased by more than six times over that same period. In FY1960, excise tax collections amounted to approximately to $355.49 billion in 2012 constant dollars. The brief spike in excise tax collection during the early 1980s was largely due to the enactment of the excise tax on windfall profits in the oil industry, which was phased-out by 1993.[39] While the number, rates, and types of excise taxes in effect have changed between 1960 and 2012, these data illustrate the declining role of excise taxes in federal public finance.

Furthermore, federal excise tax receipts as a share of gross domestic product (GDP) are lower today than they were in the past. As shown in Figure 2, annual excise tax receipts averaged between 2.0% and 2.5% during the Great Depression, before hitting a peak above 3.0% of GDP during World War II. After the end of the war, federal excise tax receipts declined as a share of GDP—particularly after the reforms in the mid-1960s. After a brief spike in the early 1980s, largely due to the enactment of the oil industry windfall profits tax, excise tax revenue as a share of GDP trended back below 1.0% by the end of the 1980s. In FY2012, federal excise tax receipts were 0.5% of GDP.

Source: Office of Management and Budget, *Budget of the United States FY2014 - Historical Tables*, Table 2.3, at http://www.whitehouse.gov/omb/budget /historicals.

Figure 2. Federal Excise Tax Receipts as a Share of Gross Domestic Product (GDP), FY1934 to FY2012.

Federal excise taxes have also declined as a share of all federal tax receipts. As shown in Figure 3, federal excise taxes comprised 45.8% of all federal tax receipts in FY1934. After the end of World War II, the share of federal tax receipts from excises began a slow decline below 15% towards a recent trend around 3.2% (in FY2012).

This decline in the share of federal tax receipts collected from excises corresponded with an increase in the role of other sources of tax receipts, notably from the individual income tax code. In 1934, individual income taxes amounted to 14.2% of all federal tax receipts and applied primarily to a narrow tax base.[40] During World War II, the individual tax code supplanted excises as being the primary source of federal revenue, as income taxes accounted for 45.0% of all tax receipts in 1944 (compared to 10.9% from excises).[41] Additionally, receipts from social insurance and retirement programs have increased over time.

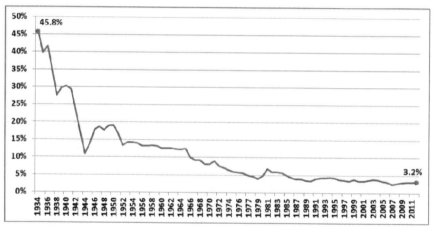

Source: Office of Management and Budget, *Budget of the United States FY2014 - Historical Tables,* Table 2.2, at http://www.whitehouse.gov/omb/budget /historicals.

Figure 3. Federal Excise Tax Receipts as a Share of All Federal Tax Receipts, FY1934 to FY2012.

Interactions between Federal and State and Local Excise Taxes

Higher federal excise tax rates tend to reduce state and local excise tax revenues derived from the same products (and *vice versa*).[42] As federal excise taxes increase the price of the targeted product, then consumer demand may decrease depending on the response of consumers.[43] This decrease in consumer demand reduces the tax base. States can increase their excise tax rates to help offset any reductions in the tax base, although higher state taxes can also drive down demand for products subject to excise taxes.

Similar to trends at the federal level, though, excise tax collections comprise a relatively small share of state and local tax revenue. As shown in Figure 4, personal property taxes were the largest source (34%) of tax revenue for state and local governments combined in 2012. Individual income taxes and general sales taxes accounted for 22% and 21% (respectively) of state and local tax collections in 2012. Excise taxes on motor fuel, tobacco, and alcohol have accounted for 5% of total tax collections.

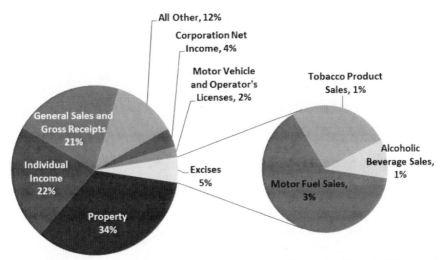

Source: CRS analysis of data from U.S. Census Bureau, Table 1 – Historical National Totals of State and Local Tax Revenue, at http://www.census.gov/govs/qtax/.

Figure 4. Sources of State and Local Tax Collections, 2012.

However, the data in Figure 4 underrepresent the amount of state tax revenue derived from tobacco sales because settlement payments from major tobacco companies to the states and territories are not included.[44] In comparison, approximately $7.3 billion in payments were made by the major tobacco companies to the states in 2011 whereas state and local tax collections from tobacco excise taxes were approximately $17.5 billion (i.e., the payments to states amounted to 41.7% of state and local excise collections).[45] Settlement payments allocated to each state and territory are largely based on tobacco consumption in that particular state or territory.

EQUITY

Economists generally measure tax equity using two measures: vertical equity and horizontal equity. Vertical equity generally implies that households with a greater ability to pay the tax (i.e., a higher income) pay a greater share of their household income in taxes than households with a lesser ability to pay the tax. A tax system is *progressive* if higher income households pay a greater share of their income in tax than lower income households, whereas the converse is true in a *regressive* tax system. Horizontal equity indicates that households with similar abilities to pay actually pay similar amounts in tax. For example, all households earning a particular amount of income would pay the same amount in taxes in a tax system with perfect horizontal equity.

Note that the excise tax rate on a particular good does not reflect its effects on equity. Even if all consumers are subject to the same tax rate of $1.00 per unit, the tax cannot be immediately deemed as "equitable" from an economic perspective. The tax's effects on equity will ultimately be a function of who bears the tax's burden.

Figure 5 shows the distribution of excise taxes paid in 2009, by average tax rates, as calculated by the Congressional Budget Office (CBO). Average tax rates represent the share of excise taxes paid as a share of pre-tax income.

With regard to vertical equity, excise taxes tend to be regressive. The lowest income quintile of taxpayers paid, on average, 1.5% of their income on excise taxes in 2009 whereas the highest quintile of taxpayers paid 0.4% of their income in excise taxes.

A luxury tax may be less regressive than other forms of excise taxes, but it could be difficult to isolate the burden of such a tax to upper-income households. First, middle-income consumers might purchase goods classified as "luxuries," such as jewelry or watches. Second, the definition of "luxury" changes over time. For example, a federal excise tax on telephone calls was first introduced in 1892 as a luxury tax to help finance the Spanish-American War. After several instances of repeal and reauthorization throughout the early 20th century, the tax remained part of the permanent tax code from 1947 until 2006.[46] Although one could make the argument in 1892 that telephone calls were "luxury" services, this was certainly not the case by the latter half of the 20th century.

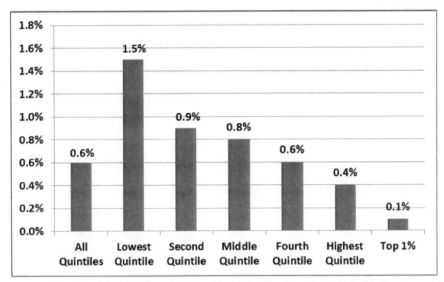

Source: Congressional Budget Office, *The Distribution of Household Income and Federal Taxes*, July 2012, pp. 27 and 33, at http://www.cbo.gov/sites /default/files/cbofiles/attachments/43373-AverageTaxRates_screen.pdf.

Notes: Average tax rates are equal to the amount of taxes paid divided by pre-tax income. The average amount of pre-tax income for each quintile in 2009 was $88,400 (all), $23,900 (lowest), $43,400 (second), $64,300 (middle), $93,800 (fourth), $223,500 (highest), and $1,219,700 (top 1%).

Figure 5. Distribution of Federal Excise Taxes, by Average Tax Rates, 2009.

With regard to horizontal equity, excise taxes have different effects on households with the same level of income. Households that consume the taxed good pay a larger share of taxes out of their current income than households that do not consume the taxed good. Excise taxes can also create horizontal inequities across consumers of a taxed product if unequal tax rates are applied to various forms of that product (e.g., beer vs. wine vs. distilled spirits).

EFFICIENCY

In short, some excise taxes are intended to affect consumer choices. As such, they reduce economic efficiency by distorting what economists characterize as economically optimal consumer behavior. This distortion could be justified, in economic terms, if there is some sort of market failure whereby the consumer's price does not capture the effect of spillover effects to society that result from consumption of the good or service. Individual consumption of certain goods and services might have negative spillover effects, or *externalities*, on society. For excise taxes intended to compensate for the social costs of certain types of consumption, economic theory suggests that the excise tax rate should be set at a level that offsets the negative costs of that consumption to society. If taxes are used this way to reflect the full cost of a particular type of economic activity to society, then excise taxes can actually lead to a more efficient allocation of resources.

General Behavioral Effects

All types of excise tax have some similar economic effects in a competitive industry.[47] In the short run, an excise tax increases the price of the taxed product (by some fraction of the tax amount), and tax burden could be shared by producers or the consumers. Next, the quantity of the product demanded is reduced. Lastly, the price received by producers for the product is also reduced (i.e., producers receive less for the product post-tax compared to pre-tax).

The exact effect depends on the responsiveness, or *elasticities*, of demand and supply for the product (or the percent change in quantity demanded or supplied, respectively, divided by the percent change in price). The increase in retail price resulting from the tax will be greater as the elasticity of supply increases and the elasticity of demand falls. The effect on quantity will be greater as both the elasticity of demand and the elasticity of supply increase.

In regard to sharing the price burden, the more inelastic the demand is, the larger the share of the tax borne by consumers. The more inelastic the supply is, the larger the share borne by producers. In the limiting cases, consumers will bear the full burden if demand is completely inelastic, whereas producers will bear the full price burden if supply is completely inelastic. Put differently, an excise tax on a product with a relatively inelastic demand will have less of an effect on consumption.[48]

Additionally, economic theory indicates that targeted excise taxes could have efficiency merits, but broadly drawn taxes that cover many product categories generally tend to lead to more distortions and reductions in economic activity than are warranted. From an efficiency perspective, the use of a broad-based tax on a wide range of activities (e.g., a general sales tax) would be preferable to a high excise tax rate on a small number of activities.[49]

Luxury Taxes

Luxury taxes are usually levied to increase progressivity in the tax system or to increase revenue, not on the basis of improving economic efficiency.

Some argue that luxury taxes in the past have dramatically reduced sales in the targeted industry. However, it is likely that demand for luxury goods is less sensitive to price changes than non-luxury goods, in part, because some luxury consumption goods are purchased by businesses rather than individuals (and could be deducted from a business's income tax returns as a business expense).

A common case study cited in the analysis of luxury taxes includes the luxury boat industry during the early 1990s. Opponents of the luxury tax argued that the yacht industry experienced drastic reductions in sales following the enactment of a 10% *ad valorem* luxury tax in the Omnibus Budget Reconciliation Act of 1990 (OBRA90). According to this logic, the imposition of the excise tax was largely to blame for the decline in sales and rise in unemployment in the industry. However, economic analysis indicates that the yacht sales were beginning to decline from their peak in 1988 (before the tax), and that sales of yachts were more sensitive to changes in personal disposable income and corporate profits after tax rather than price changes due to the tax.[50] In any case, the tax was repealed in the Omnibus Budget Reconciliation Act of 1993 (P.L. 103-66).

Sumptuary Taxes

Sumptuary tax increases are often based on market failures, relating to *externalized* costs of individual behavior associated with public health, public safety, and additional financial burdens placed on publically financed health services.[51] In short, studies measuring the respective size of the externalities for alcohol and tobacco involve very complicated, technical calculations of lifetime external costs and savings associated with alcohol and tobacco consumption that are often subject to controversy and methodological scrutiny. An advanced review of this literature is beyond the scope of this particular report. Still, studies suggest that current law per-unit tax rates on cigarettes exceed the magnitude of the estimated net externalities whereas the opposite could be true for alcohol taxes.[52]

Behavioral responses to sumptuary taxes vary by consumption good. Demand for beer is not particularly responsive to changes in price (e.g., demand is inelastic). Meta-analyses tend to find the demand for beer is more inelastic (i.e., less responsive) to changes in price than demand for either wine or distilled spirits. However, studies diverge on the question of whether demand for wine is more or less elastic than distilled spirits.[53] In comparison, CBO estimates the price elasticity of demand for cigarettes to be between (0.3) and (0.7), and that the average elasticity of the number of smokers is (0.3). In other words, a 1% increase in the price of cigarettes results in between a 0.3% and a 0.7% decrease in demand, and a 1% rise in the price of cigarettes results in roughly a 0.3% decrease in the number of smokers.[54]

Compared to a sumptuary tax on a product that is relatively elastic, a tax on a product that is relatively inelastic often results in a higher tax burden on lower-income households (due to the regressive nature of the tax) with a smaller degree of change in consumption.

Benefit-Based Taxes

If properly structured, benefit-based taxes could enhance economic efficiency by reducing the spread between private and social costs. In short, inefficiency arises because private markets tend to overproduce economic activities that lead to negative social externalities and underproduce economic activities that lead to positive externalities, absent government intervention. Theory suggests that government intervention can better incorporate social costs into the prices perceived by any one individual. However, it is often difficult to derive the "correct" tax rate that precisely accounts for the marginal social effects of an economic activity.[55]

Benefit-based taxes can affect consumer demand for public goods if the link between the tax and the use of the public good is clearly apparent. A lack of a direct link between the tax and the use of the public good could lead to declining revenues available for upkeep and maintenance of the public good. For example, one could argue that the purchase of gasoline does not necessarily lead to wear and tear on federal highways; some of this fuel could be used by drivers that commute just along local roads. Thus, many benefit-based taxes are levied on rough proxies that affect forms of consumption unrelated to the ultimate goal of the policy.

An alternative policy could include more direct forms of benefit-based taxation, but there could be a tradeoff between the targeting precision of a tax and its administrative costs. For example, although a retail tax on gasoline sales might be an imperfect proxy for highway usage, it is less complicated than administering an excise tax based on the weight and mileage of every motor vehicle using a federal highway. The costs of the latter form of tax administration might exceed the benefits.

Regulatory and Environmental Taxes

Much like benefit-based taxes, regulatory and environmental taxes are typically imposed on economic activities that generate externalities.[56] Whereas benefit-based taxes are concerned with an underproduction of some positive externality (e.g., a public good), regulatory and environmental taxes, however, are usually concerned with the overproduction of some negative externality (e.g., pollution). These negative externalities could include losses from damage to plants and animals and to their habitats, rapid deterioration to physical infrastructure, and various harmful effects on human health and mortality.

Economic theory indicates that a tax on the marginal production of these negative externalities could be used as a disincentive for harmful production processes and as a means of compensating society for the cleanup and mitigation of those externalities.

In the choice between a tax on pollution (or the regulation of some other activity with negative spillover effects on society) and a total ban on its production, economists generally prefer a tax.[57] From an economic perspective, a society's "optimum level" of pollution is usually not zero; instead, economists look to minimize total waste disposal costs. These costs could include residual waste or by-product recycling, input switching to safer materials, production modification, or other technology adoption. It can be expected that marginal pollution costs increase with increased waste disposal activities as greater investment in more advanced (and more costly) cleanup technologies and mitigation strategies is necessary. Put differently, there may be a point where the marginal cost of eliminating a particular unit of pollution may exceed the marginal benefit. The tax increases the private costs of pollution to reduce the spread between private and social costs.

To achieve optimum, economic efficiency, the excise tax rate would be set at a level such that the marginal, private cost of pollution is equal to the marginal, social benefits of production. Economic theory suggests that the tax should be imposed directly upon the activity which gives rise to the negative externality.[58]

The statutory incidence (or burden) of the tax may differ from the economic incidence, because the latter is affected by elasticities. Thus, consumers may bear some or all of the tax through higher prices.[59]

APPENDIX. REFERENCES TO CRS REPORTS ON SPECIFIC EXCISE TAXES

Affordable Care Act Taxes
*CRS CRS Report R41128, Health-Related Revenue Provisions in the Patient Protection and Affordable Care Act (ACA), by
Janemarie Mulvey
CRS Report R42971, Medical Device Excise Tax Regulations, by Andrew Nolan
Alcohol
CRS Report R41028, The Rum Excise Tax Cover-Over: Legislative History and Current Issues, by Steven Maguire
Aviation
CRS Report R42781, Federal Civil Aviation Programs: An Overview, by Bart Elias *CRS Report RS22641, Taxation of Aviation Prior to 1970, by Robert S. Kirk
Carbon Tax
CRS Report R42731, Carbon Tax: Deficit Reduction and Other Considerations, by Jonathan L. Ramseur, Jane A. Leggett, and Molly F. Sherlock CRS Report R40242, Carbon Tax and Greenhouse Gas Control: Options and Considerations for Congress, by Jonathan L. Ramseur and Larry Parker
Coal
CRS Report RS22881, Coal Excise Tax Refunds: United States v. Clintwood Elkhorn Mining Co., by Erika K. Lunder *CRS Report RS21935, The Black Lung Excise Tax on Coal, by Salvatore Lazzari
Gasoline
CRS Report R40808, The Role of Federal Gasoline Excise Taxes in Public Policy, by Robert Pirog CRS Report R42877, Funding and Financing Highways and Public Transportation, by Robert S. Kirk and William J. Mallett *CRS Report RL30304, The Federal Excise Tax on Gasoline and the Highway Trust Fund: A Short History, by James M. Bickley
Guns and Ammunition
CRS Report R42992, Guns, Excise Taxes, and Wildlife Restoration, by M. Lynne Corn and Jane G. Gravelle
Oil Industry
CRS Report RL34689, Oil Industry Financial Performance and the Windfall Profits Tax, by Robert Pirog and Molly F. Sherlock CRS Report R43128, Oil Sands and the Oil Spill Liability Trust Fund: The Definition of "Oil" and Related Issues for Congress, by Jonathan L. Ramseur
Rubber Tires
*CRS Report RL30302, Federal Excise Tax on Tires: Where the Rubber Meets the Road, by Pamela J. Jackson
Sea Commerce, Harbor Maintenance, Boating, and Inland Waterways

CRS Report R41042, Harbor Maintenance Trust Fund Expenditures, by John Frittelli CRS Report RS22060, The Sport Fish Restoration and Boating Trust Fund, by Eugene H. Buck and M. Lynne Corn CRS Report R41430, Inland Waterways: Recent Proposals and Issues for Congress, by Charles V. Stern

Tobacco
CRS Report R40226, P.L. 111-3: The Children's Health Insurance Program Reauthorization Act of 2009, by Evelyne P. Baumrucker, Elicia J. Herz, and Jane G. Gravelle *CRS Report RS22681, The Cigarette Tax Increase to Finance SCHIP, by Jane G. Gravelle *CRS Report 97-1053, The Proposed Tobacco Settlement: Who Pays for the Health Costs of Smoking?, by Jane G. Gravelle *CRS Report 94-214, Cigarette Taxes to Fund Health Care Reform: An Economic Analysis, by Jane G. Gravelle and Dennis Zimmerman

Source: http://www.crs.gov/.

Notes: Archived reports are denoted with an [*]. Archived reports are available on the CRS webpage, but may not contain the most recent data on a particular tax. Authors of some archived reports may no longer be available at CRS.

End Notes

[1] This list is not exhaustive. For example, rationing taxes have been temporarily levied in order to reduce the consumption of critical supplies during wartime (e.g., rubber) and import duties are basically excise taxes levied on imports generally to protect domestic industries.

[2] Economists also refer to taxes applied to an activity generating negative externalities as a "Pigovian tax." This type of tax is named after economist Arthur Pigou, who developed the concept of economic externalities.

[3] Excise taxes were previously imposed on luxury vehicles, furs, yachts, etc. However, most of these provisions have either expired or have been repealed over the years.

[4] Economists generally do not view job creation as a justification for providing federal assistance to certain industries in the long run. They argue that in the long run such assistance will likely reallocate jobs within the economy, not increase them. In their view, jobs arise primarily from the size of the labor force.

[5] For a comprehensive list of federal excise taxes and their tax rates (as of 2011), see U.S. Congress, Joint Committee on Taxation, Present Law and Background Information on Federal Excise Tax Rates, committee print, 112th Cong., 1st sess., January 2011, JCS-1-11 (Washington: GPO, 2011). The JCT study classifies some provisions as "excise taxes," although these penalties are often thought of as "penalties" for certain types of behavior (e.g., the Patient Protection and Affordable Care Act's penalty for employers who do not provide "adequate" and "affordable" health care coverage to their employees).

[6] For an earlier history of federal excise taxes, see Tax Foundation, *Federal Excise Taxes*, June 1, 1956, at http://taxfoundation.org/article/federal-excise-taxes.

[7] For a more in-depth history of federal excise taxes, archived CRS reports are available from the author upon request.

[8] Steve Simon, "Alexander Hamilton and the Whiskey Tax," U.S. Department of the Treasury, http://www.ttb.gov/ public_info/special_feature.shtml.

[9] Tax Foundation, *Federal Excise Taxes*, June 1, 1956, p.9, at http://taxfoundation.org/article /federal-excise-taxes.

[10] Robert L. Einhorn, *American Taxation, American Slavery* (Chicago, IL: University of Chicago Press, 2008); and Joel S. Newman, "Slave Tax as Sin Tax: 18th and 19th Century Perspectives," *Tax Notes*, November 21, 2003.

[11] Tax Foundation, *Federal Excise Taxes*, June 1, 1956, p.9, at http://taxfoundation.org/article/federal-excise-taxes.

[12] The Revenue Act of 1861 also temporarily imposed the first income tax, which was implemented in 1862. The income tax was repealed in 1872.

[13] By comparison, trade tariffs produced from one-half to two-thirds of all revenue in the decades after the Civil War, whereas proceeds from federal land sales accounted primarily for the remainder of revenue collections. See Lance E. Davis and John Legler, "The Government in the American Economy, 1815-1902: A Quantitative Study," *The Journal of Economic History*, vol. 26, no. 4 (December 1966), pp. 514-552.

[14] During parts of this period of time, only customs duties outnumbered excise tax collections as the primary source of federal revenue.

[15] Tax Foundation, *Federal Excise Taxes*, June 1, 1956, p.11, at http://taxfoundation.org/article/federal-excise-taxes.

[16] See Table 3 in Tax Foundation, *Federal Excise Taxes*, June 1, 1956, p.14, at http://taxfoundation.org/article/federalexcise-taxes.

[17] See Revenue Act of 1940 (P.L. 76-656), Revenue Act of 1941 (P.L. 77-250), Revenue Act of 1942 (P.L. 77-753), and Revenue Act of 1943 (P.L. 78-235); and Tax Foundation, *Federal Excise Taxes*, June 1, 1956, p.17, at http://taxfoundation.org/article/federal-excise-taxes.

[18] See W.C. Bryant, "Key Republicans Toss Political Dynamite Into Laps of Leaders: Ask Excise Tax Raise," *Wall Street Journal*, October 21, 1947, p. 5.

[19] U.S. Congress, Senate Committee on Finance, *Senate Report on the Excise Tax Reduction Act of 1965*, 89th Cong., 1st sess., June 14, 1965, S. Rpt. 89-324 (Washington: GPO, 1965), p. 1. Although many of the scheduled reductions and taxes repealed by the act were delayed until the late 1960s and early 1970s. See Joseph Pechman, *Federal Tax Policy*, 3rd ed. (Washington, DC: Brookings Institution Press, 1977), p. 189.

[20] See R. Rudy Higgins-Evenson, "Financing for a Second Era of Internal Improvements," *Social Science History*, vol. 26, no. 4 (Winter 2002), pp. 623-651.

[21] For more information on financing public highways, see CRS Report R42877, *Funding and Financing Highways and Public Transportation*, by Robert S. Kirk and William J. Mallett.

[22] Congressional interest in enacting consumption taxes has been low. For example, a type of national consumption tax, a value-added-tax, has been explicitly rejected by Congress in the past. The Senate voted 85-13 on a resolution rejecting a value-added-tax (VAT) in 2010. See S.Amdt. 3724 (111th).

[23] The Congressional Budget Office (CBO) estimated in 2008 that tax on sugar sweetened beverages set at 3 cents per 12 ounces could raise $50.4 million in revenue in five years. In 2011, CBO estimated that a tax on greenhouse gas emissions could raise nearly $1.2 trillion over 10 years. See CBO, *Budget Options Volume 1: Health Care*, December 2008, p. 192, at http://www.cbo.gov/sites/default/files/cbofiles/ftpdocs/99xx/doc9925/12-18-health options.pdf; and CBO, *Reducing the Deficit: Spending and Revenue Options*, March 2011, p. 205, at http://www.cbo.gov/sites/default/ files/cbofiles/ftpdocs/120xx/doc12085/03-10-reducingthedeficit.pdf.

[24] Sijbren Cnossen, *Excise Systems: A Global Study of the Selective Taxation of Goods and Services* (Baltimore, MD: Johns Hopkins University Press, 1977), p. 10.

[25] If taxes are used this way to reflect the full cost of a particular type of economic activity to society, then excise taxes can actually lead to a more efficient allocation of resources. This concept is discussed in more detail in the "Efficiency" section of this report.

[26] For more information on excise taxes on firearms and ammunition see CRS Report R42992, *Guns, Excise Taxes, and Wildlife Restoration*, by M. Lynne Corn and Jane G. Gravelle.

[27] The decline in the real value of per unit taxes is due, in part, to increasing real prices of the taxed commodity or activity over time.

[28] A proof gallon is a combination of alcohol content and volume. A proof gallon is the volume in gallons, multiplied by the percent alcohol, multiplied by two, and divided by 100.

[29] U.S. Department of the Treasury, Alcohol and Tobacco Tax and Trade Bureau, at http://www.ttb.gov/tax_audit/ atftaxes.shtml.

[30] CRS calculations based on Consumer Price Index for All Urban Consumers (CPI-U) for all items at http://www.bls.gov/cpi/data.htm (accessed May 23, 2013).

[31] Sijbren Cnossen, *Excise Systems: A Global Study of the Selective Taxation of Goods and Services* (Baltimore, MD: Johns Hopkins University Press, 1977), p. 15.

[32] Center for Disease Control and Prevention, "Economic Facts About U.S. Tobacco Production and Use," at http://www.cdc.gov/tobacco/data_statistics/fact_sheets/economics/econ_facts/.

[33] For more information, see CRS Report R42992, *Guns, Excise Taxes, and Wildlife Restoration*, by M. Lynne Corn and Jane G. Gravelle.

[34] Alternatively, the manufacturer could have invested the money used to pay the tax and earned a market rate of return during the period between when it paid the tax and when the good is sold along the next step of the production chain.

[35] For more information, see Internal Revenue Service, *Farmer's Tax Guide* (Publication 225), Chapter 14 – Excise Taxes, at http://www.irs.gov/publications/p225/ch14.html.

[36] CCH, Tax Research Consultant, "Excise: 100, Fundamental Concepts: Federal Excise Taxes," accessed via Intelliconnect research database on 8/12/2013.

[37] Because these calculations control for changes in the price level, economists generally compare dollar-denominated amounts over time in real terms, not nominal.

[38] For particular federal "trust funds" that are financed through excise taxes, the decline in the value of excise tax revenue can be of a concern. If the growth in spending exceeds revenue, then the trust fund could be depleted over time.

[39] Crude Oil Windfall Profit Tax Act of 1980 (P.L. 96-223).

[40] Office of Management and Budget, *Budget of the United States FY2014 - Historical Tables*, Table 2.2, at http://www.whitehouse.gov/omb/budget/historicals.

[41] The rise in income tax receipts during World War II was largely due to the enactment of the "Victory Tax" under the Revenue Act of 1942 (P.L. 77-753). The Victory Tax was a flat 5% tax (lowered to 3% in 1943) on net income over $624, with few deductions. The Individual Income Tax Act of 1944 (P.L. 78-315) repealed the Victory Tax but also raised the marginal tax rates set in statute under the individual income tax code. For more information, see Roy G. Blakey and Gladys C. Blakey, "The Federal Revenue Act of 1942," *American Political Science Review*, vol. 36, no. 6 (December 1942), pp. 1069-1082; Roy G. Blakey and Gladys C. Blakey, "Federal Revenue Legislation, 1943-1944," *American Political Science Review*, vol. 38, no. 2 (April 1944), pp. 325-330; and Paul G. Kauper, "Significant Developments in the Law of Federal Taxation, 1941-1947: I," *Michigan Law Review*, vol. 45, no. 6 (April 1947), pp. 659-678.

[42] The actual magnitude of this effect is difficult to measure, as state and local governments have also raised excise taxes over time.

[43] These behavioral responses, or elasticities, are discussed more in the "Efficiency" section of this report.

[44] In 1998, the Attorneys General of 46 states signed the Master Settlement Agreement (MSA) with the four largest tobacco companies in the United States to settle state and territorial suits to recover billions of dollars in costs associated with treating smoking-related illnesses. Four states (Florida, Minnesota, Mississippi, and Texas) settled their tobacco

cases separately from the MSA states. In short, MSA funds are allocated to the states and territories according to a formula based on estimated tobacco-related Medicaid expenditures and the number of smokers in each state and territory. The annual payments are subject to a number of adjustments, reductions, and offsets—particularly a volumeof-sales adjustment. In other words, the MSA payments are based, in part, on tobacco consumption by state or territory. For more information see National Association of Attorneys General (NAAG), "NAAG Tobacco Project," at http://www.naag.org/tobacco.php.

[45] For tobacco settlement payments to the states data, see Campaign for Tobacco-Free Kids, *Actual Tobacco Settlement Payments Received by the States, 2002-2012*, October 2012, at http://www.tobaccofreekids.org/research/factsheets/pdf/ 0365.pdf; for state and local excise tax collections data see U.S. Census Bureau, Table 1 – Historical National Totals of State and Local Tax Revenue, at http://www.census.gov/govs/qtax/.

[46] The federal tax on telephone calls was imposed temporarily from 1892 to 1902 to raise revenue to help finance the Spanish-American War. The "telephone tax" was temporarily imposed again from 1917 to 1924 to help finance U.S. efforts in World War I. The tax was reintroduced temporarily in 1932 to finance the government during the recovery from the Great Depression, and was temporarily extended until its "permanent" authorization from 1947 until 2006. For a history of the telephone tax, see Joseph J. Thorndike, "The Phone Tax: Gone but Never Forgotten," *Tax Notes*, June 1, 2006.

[47] J. Fred Giertz, "Excise Taxes," in *Encyclopedia of Taxation and Tax Policy*, ed. Joseph J. Cordes, Robert D. Ebel, and Jane G. Gravelle, 2nd ed. (Urban Institute Press, 2000). Economists also refer to competitive markets as exhibiting "pure competition," where no single participant (buyer or seller) has enough power to affect the market price of a product. In contrast, sellers in markets characterized by a single or small group of sellers with enough power to affect prices (i.e., a monopoly or oligopoly) may be able to pass more of the cost of the tax along to consumers in the form of higher prices.

[48] The magnitude of the elasticity is sometimes reported and the negative sign omitted because consumer demand is often negatively correlated with prices. The important factor is if the elasticity is less than or greater than "1." Consumer goods with an elasticity greater than "1" are considered price elastic; less than "1," price inelastic. The elasticity of demand is not necessarily constant along all price points. Economic theory indicates that consumer demand is relatively more inelastic in the short run and with larger changes in price than with smaller changes in price. In the long run, however, elasticity of demand for a product is relatively elastic as consumers adjust their behavior to changes in prices.

[49] In economic terms, this concept relates to the growth of "deadweight losses" (or "excess burdens") associated with the tax. The excess burdens of an excise tax increase roughly with the square of the tax rate (e.g., doubling the tax rate quadruples the welfare loss). See J. Fred Giertz, "Excise Taxes," in *Encyclopedia of Taxation and Tax Policy*, ed. Joseph J. Cordes, Robert D. Ebel, and Jane G. Gravelle, 2nd ed. (Washington, DC: Urban Institute Press, 2002).

[50] This analysis is contained in CRS Report 92-149, *The Effect of the Luxury Excise Tax on the Sale of Luxury Boats*, by Dennis Zimmerman. This 1992 report is available upon request from the author of this report.

[51] With regard to correcting for negative externalities, regulation can also serve as an alternative (or complementary) policy to taxation.

[52] For the most comprehensive summary of this analysis, see archived CRS Report 94-214, *Cigarette Taxes to Fund Health Care Reform: An Economic Analysis*, by Jane G. Gravelle and Dennis Zimmerman, particularly pp. 3-6. The analysis in this CRS report is largely

based on the findings of study commission by the RAND Corporation. See Willard G. Manning et al., The Costs of Poor Health Habits (Cambridge, MA: Harvard University Press, 1991). For additional support, see Congressional Budget Office, Federal Taxation of Tobacco, Alcoholic Beverages, and Motor Fuels, August 1990, p. 47, at http://www.cbo.gov/sites/default/files/cbofiles/ftpdocs/79xx/doc7951/90-cbo-039.pdf. These studies were conducted before further increases in federal, state, and local excise taxes on cigarettes and the 1998 settlements between the major tobacco companies and the states and territories.

[53] For two examples of studies that indicate that distilled spirits are more elastic than wine, see James Fogarty, "The Demand for Beer, Wine and Spirits: A Survey of the Literature," Journal of Economic Surveys, vol. 24, no. 3 (2010), pp. 428-478; and Alexander C. Wagenaar, Matthew J. Salois, and Kelli A. Komro, "Effects of Beverage Alcohol Price and Tax Levels on Drinking: A Meta-Analysis of 1003 Estimates from 112 Studies," Addiction, vol. 104, no. 2 (2009), pp. 179-190. For an example of a study that indicates that wine is more elastic than distilled spirits, see Craig A. Gallet, "The Demand for Alcohol: A Meta-Analysis of Elasticities," The Australian Journal of Agricultural and Resource Economics, vol. 51, no. 2 (June 2007), pp. 121-135; and See Congressional Budget Office, Federal Taxation of Tobacco, Alcoholic Beverages, and Motor Fuels, August 1990, p. 72, at http://www.cbo.gov/sites/default/files/cbofiles/ ftpdocs/79xx/doc7951/90-cbo-039.pdf.

[54] Congressional Budget Office, Raising the Excise Tax on Cigarettes: Effects on Health and the Federal Budget, June 2012, p. vi, at http://www.cbo.gov/publication/43319.

[55] For more discussion of these issues, see Harvey S. Rosen, Public Finance, 7th ed. (New York, NY: McGraw-Hill, 2005), p. 93.

[56] For more background on environmental taxes, see Maureen L. Cropper and Wallace E. Oates, "Environmental Economics: A Survey," Journal of Economic Literature, vol. 30, no. 2 (June 1992), pp. 675-740.

[57] In theory, negative environmental and regulatory externalities could be mitigated with policies other than a tax, such as production quotas or tradable permits. Each policy option has its own advantages and disadvantages, particularly with regard to setting the price of the tax or permit or the level of the quota. For a more in-depth comparison of these policies, see A. Lans Bovenberg and Lawrence H. Goulder, Environmental Taxation and Regulation, National Bureau of Economic Research, NBER Working Paper 8458, September 2001, at http://www.nber.org/papers/w8458.pdf; and Don Fullerton, Andrew Leicester, and Stephen Smith, Environmental Taxes, National Bureau of Economic Research, NBER Working Paper 14197, July 2008, at http://www.nber.org/papers/w14197.pdf; and Frank S. Arnold, Why Policy Makers Don't Use Environmental Taxes, draft report prepared under cooperative agreement with the U.S. Environmental Protection Agency, January 6, 1994, at http://yosemite.epa.gov/ee/epa/eerm.nsf/vwAN/EE-0312-1.pdf/ $file/EE-0312-1.pdf.

[58] For more information, see Thomas A. Barthold, "Issues in the Design of Environmental Excise Taxes," The Journal of Economic Perspectives, vol. 8, no. 1 (Winter 1994), pp. 133-151.

[59] A more elastic demand (supply) indicates that consumers (producers) are more responsive to changes in price. Consumers absorb a larger share of the tax when producer supply is more elastic than consumer demand.

INDEX

J

L

M

S

T